Contents

List of contributors   vii
Acknowledgements   viii
Introduction   ix

PART ONE   *Interpersonal Behaviour*   1

1   *Secure Systems*   3
     RON LUDLOW
2   *The Giro Group*   8
     PAUL DAINTY
3   *Kleine Plastics*   17
     RON LUDLOW
4   *Henry Smart*   28
     RON LUDLOW
5, 6   *Peter Johnson and Maurice Bradley*   35
     DAVID BUTCHER AND CATHERINE BAILEY
7   *The Industrial Development Authority*   48
     ANDREW P. KAKABADSE
8   *Guy Roberts*   57
     RON LUDLOW
9   *Grayle Engineering*   62
     RON LUDLOW
10   *The Youth Training Scheme*   70
     RON LUDLOW

PART TWO   *Strategic Management*   75

11   *The Syntax Corporation*   77
     ANDREW P. KAKABADSE
12   *The box makers: the case of SafePAC plc*   111
     ANDREW P. KAKABADSE
13   *The Celtic Woollen Company*   120
     ANDREW P. KAKABADSE

Contents

14 The Public Welfare Agency   129
    JACQUELINE DRAKE AND ANDREW P. KAKABADSE
15 Fosbar Electronics   146
    RON LUDLOW
16 Olde England Taverns   153
    TIM NORMAN AND JACQUELINE DRAKE
17 The Epicurus Leisure Group   169
    SHAUN TYSON

PART THREE Personnel Planning and Systems   175

18 Pallas Electronics   177
    JOHN BERESFORD AND SHAUN TYSON
19 Archon Engineering   182
    SHAUN TYSON
20 Lysander Products   188
    SHAUN TYSON
21 Thomas Nestor Limited (Printers)   194
    SHAUN TYSON
22 Recruiting a national sales force   200
    FERGUS PANTON

PART FOUR Employee Relations   207

23 East Midland Electronic   209
    ROGER JONES
24 A case of piecework bargaining   215
    ROGER JONES
25 BIFU: a problem of union structure and democracy   221
    PAUL WILLMAN
26 Greenfield Industrial   226
    PAUL WILLMAN
27 Suspending quality circles: Alcan Plate Limited   230
    JOHN BANK

Index   241

Cases in Human Resource Management: Teachers' Case Guide

Cases in Human Resource Management: Teachers' Case Guide

EDITED BY

SHAUN TYSON AND
ANDREW P. KAKABADSE

HEINEMANN : LONDON

William Heinemann Ltd
10 Upper Grosvenor Street, London W1X 9PA

LONDON   MELBOURNE   JOHANNESBURG   AUCKLAND

First published 1987
© William Heinemann Ltd 1987

British Library Cataloguing in Publication Data
Cases in human resource management:
teachers' case guide.
1. Personnel management – Case studies
I. Tyson, Shaun   II. Kakabadse, Andrew
658.3′00722   HF5549

ISBN 0 434 91021 X

Photoset by Wilmaset, Birkenhead, Wirral
Printed and bound in Great Britain by
Redwood Burn Limited, Trowbridge, Wiltshire

Contributors

Catherine Bailey, Freelance Consultant.

John Bank, Lecturer in Industrial Relations, Cranfield School of Management.

John Beresford, Lecturer in Statistics, Civil Service College, Sunningdale.

David Butcher, Lecturer in Organizational Behaviour, Cranfield School of Management.

Paul Dainty, Tutor in Human Resources, European School of Management Studies.

Jacqueline Drake, Lecturer in Organizational Behaviour, Cranfield School of Management.

Roger Jones, Lecturer in Industrial Relations, Cranfield School of Management.

Andrew P. Kakabadse, Professor of Management Development, Cranfield School of Management.

Ron Ludlow, Lecturer in Organizational Behaviour, Cranfield School of Management.

Tim Norman, Manager, Bank of America.

Fergus Panton, Consultant in Human Resource Management.

Shaun Tyson, Senior Lecturer in Personnel Management, Cranfield School of Management.

Paul Willman, Lecturer in Organizational Behaviour, London Business School.

Acknowledgements

We would like to acknowledge the contribution made by the hundreds of managers who have helped to shape these cases by their comments, when the cases have been taught in class. We are grateful for the help of Tony Kipperberger and Jean Bartlett in writing the Henry Smart, Grayle Engineering and Guy Roberts cases. We would also like to thank the people depicted here, or whose situations are described. Without them we can truly say there would not have been a book.

Sections of the 'Box Makers' case appear in *Working in Organisations* by A. Kakabadse, R. Ludlow and S. Vinnicombe, published by Gower 1987. The Epicurus Group', 'Archon Engineering' and 'Thomas Nestor' cases were quoted in *Evaluating the Personnel Function* by S. Tyson and A. Fell, published by Hutchinson 1986. We are grateful for permission to publish them here. The New York Times has kindly given permission for the reproduction of the article attached to the Greenfields case.

Finally, we would like to thank Dorothy Rogers and Mairi Bryce for their patience and their typing skills.

Shaun Tyson
Andrew Kakabadse

Introduction

ANDREW P. KAKABADSE

Using the *Teachers' Case Guide*

Two separate elements need to be considered in effectively using the Teachers' Case Guide:

1 Structure of the *Teachers' Case Guide*.
2 'Add-on' case parts.

Structure of the *Teachers' Case Guide*

Each case guide is divided into six parts: introduction; theory and background; key learning points; teaching guide summary; teaching style and, wherever relevant, references or a further reading guide.

The *introduction* identifies the key learning points that are covered by the case. In addition, and for the majority of cases, the particular areas of managerial and organizational behaviour on which the case focuses, are identified.

In the *theory and background* section, an analysis is provided of the underlying conceptual framework to the case. Where appropriate, references are offered which are intended to be of value to both faculty and participants.

Particular attention needs to be paid to the *key learning points*. They act as the heart to the *Teachers' Case Guide*. Each of the key learning points per case is listed and then discussed in further detail. Emphasis is given as to how to teach each of the learning points. Further, the parts of each case which can be used as examples to typify each of the learning points or subpoints, are clearly indicated.

The *teaching guide summary* offers in 'bullet point' format each of the key learning points which needs to be drawn out in the discussion of the case. The summary can be transferred on to acetate and slide projector and presented to the participant groups at the end of the discussion in order to ensure that the important principles in the case are appreciated.

Attention is paid to the manner in which each case is taught. Although original pieces of work, each of these cases has repeatedly been used in the lecture room. The guidance offered under the section, *teaching style*, represents our cumulative experience of how to teach the case in the most effective manner.

Finally, key *references* and *further reading* are placed at the end of most of the teaching case guides, which can be used by the presenter to familiarize him/herself with the topic area, or can be offered to the participant groups for further reading.

Add-ons

The following cases, *Kleine Plastics*, *Peter Johnson*, *Maurice Bradley*, *The Syntax Corporation* and *The Public Welfare Agency*, involve sequentially taught separate parts to the case, which other than Part 1 of the case, are not available in the book of cases, but are placed in the *Teachers' Case Guide*. It is intended that the case presenter copy the necessary parts so as to distribute them to the participants. As a consequence, the guide to these cases provides special instruction on the teaching of the case.

The cases of *Peter Johnson* and *Maurice Bradley* are to be treated as role play exercises and, hence, separate briefs are offered, with the brief for the boss in the case study book. The appropriate brief should be given to each of the participants involved in the role play without disclosing what is contained in the other brief, so as to effectively conduct the role play.

With *The Syntax Corporation* and *The Public Welfare Agency*, teaching notes for distribution to the participants are provided at the end of each case part discussion. The intention is that the teaching notes as well as the discussion of the case, prompt the participants to consider accurately the next steps to take in the subsequent part of the case. By breaking down complex concepts into more discrete components, it is hoped that effective learning takes place on an incremental basis.

For *Kleine Plastics*, cumulatively noting the participants' responses to the questions in each case part, and then entering the case presentation, similar to the other non add-on cases, is the procedure to follow.

Introduction

Nature of the cases

Each of these cases is directly or indirectly based on the first hand experiences of the writers, either as researchers or consultants. Although the true identity of both organization and individual employees are well hidden in order to maintain confidentiality, every attempt has been made to accurately record managerial and organizational processes. Depending on the situation, circumstances and the key issues to be learned, the cases differ in size and teaching style, and hence, not all neatly fit into one-hour lecture unit blocks. Certain cases, such as *Olde England Taverns* and *The Public Welfare Agency* require 3½ to 4 hours to complete; *The Syntax Corporation* can require one working day to read, discuss and analyse.

Therefore these cases would probably find more favour with post graduate and post experience participants who can relate the managerial and organizational processes in the case, and to their own working experiences. It is intended that the case presenter encourage discussion of such work experiences so that the learning from the case be applied back in the workplace. In this way, the cases in this book are being utilized as we the editors intended, namely that academic learning be combined with application in the workplace.

PART ONE

Interpersonal Behaviour

ONE

Secure Systems

RON LUDLOW

Introduction

The case of Secure Systems examines the factors that affect motivation and performance in work organizations. It can be used to help managers identify individual levels of motivation, and to design programmes to increase individual motivation, recognizing situational differences.

Theory and background

Many factors and forces influence individual behaviour in specific situations. One way of interpreting these behaviours is to consider that people take actions to satisfy specific needs that exist for them in those situations. Some of these needs are activated by external states and some by internal drives. External states may be such things as the weather, the environment, other people, for example, if it is raining, we want to keep dry, so we open an umbrella.

Internal drives, which may be instinctive or learnt, conscious or unconscious, may force us to behave in certain ways because of our physical, psychological, and social needs. Maslow developed a concept of motivation as a series of internal drives to satisfy an ascending hierarchy of needs. He identified these needs in ascending order as: survival, for example physiological, security, social, ego or esteem, and self-fulfilment. Higher order needs become more important to the extent that lower needs become satisfied.

One other way of looking at motivation is to consider the motivational process in organizations. People put effort into their performance because they expect that certain levels of performance will be recognized and rewarded by the organization. There are of course moderating factors to this concept, for example the know-ledge and skills of the individual employee, and a supportive environment within the organization to enable them to perform at the level which they expect. This implies that the incentives offered by the organization should attempt as nearly as possible to match the satisfaction of the individual's need in organizations to ensure high performance. As however there are great variances in individual needs in an organization, it is very difficult for organizations to apply in general the incentive schemes which will satisfy everyone.

Key learning points

1 Needs and motivation.
2 The motivational process in organizations.
3 Motivational programmes.

Needs and motivation

In the case of Secure Systems, Bill Johnson joined the company ten months ago from a major software house. In that software house the needs which had been satisfied by the organization were certainly those of existence and security (he had a good salary), and it is probable that his social needs were also satisfied to a certain extent. His ego needs were satisfied only by the status and prestige of a pleasant office and good secretarial back-up, and his self-fulfilment needs were clearly unsatisfied – 'he felt restricted and he'd steadily become more frustrated' because his creative genius was not recognized. His need for self-fulfilment had become more important because of the comparative satisfaction of the lower order needs. He felt also that the constraining structure, i.e. its bureaucracy, was also stifling his opportunities to achieve self-fulfilment.

Secure Systems gave Bill Johnson the opportunity he had been looking for to develop his innovative ability and skills. He had a challenging job, an exciting project, and he achieved self-fulfilment while he was totally immersed in the task itself. The job was so challenging that it outweighed the deprivation of some of his lower order needs. People can work at this level for so long, but when his self-fulfilment needs cease to become satisfied at the end of the project, Bill Johnson's lower order needs became more important and became motivators. He realized that his ego and esteem needs were not being satisfied by the quality of his work surroundings. His social needs were not satisfied by his constant interactions with the sardonic Leslie Jones. These ego and social needs therefore became the major internal drives in Bill Johnson's work life. The satisfaction of these needs became paramount.

The motivational process in organizations

In his previous job, Bill Johnson had expended a certain level of effort producing an adequate level of performance to achieve certain rewards and satisfaction from his organization. The incentives offered by the organization for high performance were mostly those of salary and status, i.e. extrinsic reward over which Bill Johnson had no control. The intrinsic reward which Bill Johnson was looking for was that of being able to use his creative genius, his innovative ability and skills. Because that organization did not offer the intrinsic reward he was looking for, he became steadily more frustrated and the effort which he put into his job steadily reduced with his increasing level of frustration. His job satisfaction therefore was limited.

On moving to Secure Systems, Bill Johnson still received a similar salary, but he also gained the intrinsic reward of self-fulfilment i.e. the opportunity to use his innovative talents. Consequently the effort and commitment which he put into his new job was extremely high; that is to say he was highly motivated, and he had a high level of job satisfaction. These rewards more than compensated for the loss of a different extrinsic reward which he had in his previous employment, that is, status in the form of a pleasant office and good secretarial back-up.

When, however, the intrinsic reward of self-fulfilment was reduced at the end of his project, his job satisfaction level dropped, and he looked for ways in which to increase this level of satisfaction to the level it had been during the course of the project. The extrinsic reward of status and prestige therefore became more important to him as a means of bringing his job satisfaction up to its previous level. As the motivating potential of the content of his job became lower, as he steadily got locked into a standard office routine, the contextual factors of his job and work environment became much more important to Bill Johnson. The contextual factors e.g. pay, security, social, supervisory, working conditions need to be perceived by the individual as being equitable before the motivating factors of the job content can act as motivators.

Teaching guide summary

Issues	*Learning points*
1 Needs and motivation.	<ul><li>Influences of behaviour in the work situation.</li><li>Perception of situation.</li><li>Personal value systems.</li><li>Motivation.</li><li>Need satisfaction.</li><li>Hierarchy of needs: physiological and survival security social ego and esteem self-fulfilment.</li><li>Past experiences.</li><li>Transitions.</li><li>Current situations.</li><li>Interpersonal relationships.</li><li>Reward systems/incentives.</li><li>External states.</li><li>Internal drives.</li></ul>
2 The motivational process in organizations.	<ul><li>Expectancy theory.</li><li>Equity versus equality.</li><li>Effort and ability.</li><li>Extrinsic/intrinsic rewards.</li><li>Effort → performance → rewards → satisfaction → feedback → effort . . .</li><li>Feedback.</li><li>Job design.</li></ul>
3 Motivational programmes	<ul><li>Relate motivational programmes to levels of needs at which employees are working: e.g. existence – working conditions, pay, job security. e.g. social – cohesive work groups, autonomous work groups, social activities, group harmony, group incentive schemes.</li></ul>

> e.g. growth and develop-
> ment – job redesign, job
> enrichment, job enlarge-
> ment, greater individual
> autonomy, personal deve-
> lopment, management
> development.

Teaching style

Make available white boards/black boards and flip charts for each individual group.

Ask the groups to present the results of their discussion of each question to the rest of the class. Collate on the white board/black board the key findings of each group. Fit the findings into the structure of the teaching guide. Relate the findings to need, process, and expectancy theory of motivation. Consider closely the possible actions that can be taken to improve Bill Johnson's motivation now and relate those motivational problems to the students' own work environments.

In the closing summary of the case, highlight the need that managers must be sensitive to the differences in needs that exist in their subordinates, and must attempt to ensure that their employees perceive that they are being treated fairly and equitably. Emphasize also that motivation is only one factor in achieving effective performance; that the performance equation is performance equates to ability × motivation (effort) × support (work environment).

TWO

The Giro Group

PAUL DAINTY

Introduction

The case of The Giro Group examines problems of motivation and management development. It is specifically related to the difficulties of motivating and developing managers within a contracting/ shrinking organization, or one that is stagnating. It can be used to explore these issues both from the organization's viewpoint, and also from the individual's perspective. Thus in terms of the organization, the case is meant to highlight problems of motivation, of management development, of how a company tries to manage its managerial resources overall, of the kind of management structure a company should have, and the implication this may have for morale, motivation and long-term effectiveness. In terms of the individual, the case can be used to explore personal coping and development strategies. While the case emphasizes a contracting work environment, many of the issues raised are applicable to any organizational environment.

Theory and background

The case is based on a research study of five large contracting/ shrinking manufacturing companies, which investigated the problems faced by managers in such circumstances.

Much of the motivation and management development literature, and indeed the literature on organizations in general, is written with an underlying assumption of organizational growth. However, this literature may not be appropriate to trying to tackle problems in organizations which are shrinking. In growing organizations, readapting to changing markets brings, at worst, short-term discomfort and often results in the majority of individuals gaining as a result of the organization's adjustment to the changed environment. In contracting organizations the benefits are much less positive and change here is more likely to leave the majority with circumstances less attractive than before. In these situations a company will have less money, either to allocate as formal rewards, or to devote to management development activities, fewer promotion opportunities and fewer opportunities to place managers in positions where they can gain additional experience. Some individuals will experience cuts in pay and benefits, while for others the consequences may be more severe including demotion and redundancy, but few will escape from being affected in some way or another.

Companies in these circumstances face major human resource management issues and a number of dilemmas. One dilemma is how to cut costs yet maintain management effectiveness and motivation. In these circumstances, such things as monetary rewards and management development, often seen as a 'soft' activity not directly related to the immediate problems a company faces, may be severely pruned.

A second dilemma is between creating promotion opportunities, as against maintaining the 'management structure'. Promotion is both a motivator and a potential developer of managers, yet companies may often reduce career opportunities in order to maintain some kind of stability within a company through protecting managerial jobs. Such a 'humane' policy of minimizing managerial redundancies, especially of older and less able managers, has to be weighed against the frustration caused among managers lower down in the hierarchy seeing their career opportunities blocked. Their possible resignation may leave a management structure detrimental to a company in the long term.

However, the difficulties are not only to be found with the 'organization'. Resistance and apathy towards management development, for instance, may be as equally evident among managers themselves. Managers remaining in a company after redundancy are the ones who survived. Having survived, the need for development and the need to assess strengths and weaknesses may not seem very pertinent. But being blind to personal weaknesses may also reduce awareness of other threats. In particular, political activity such as 'backstabbing', 'crawling', and plain lying may come much to the fore in organizations that are contracting. Thus, assessments of whether a person is motivated, effective, able etc., may be distorted by misinformation, prejudice, hasty judgements, and sometimes deliberate attempts to undermine individuals.

Key learnings points

Thus, a contracting environment demands a difference in emphasis to that of a growing environment; differences which can be explored through the case study. The first point is that the environment should not be seen as debilitating or as a scapegoat for inactivity, but that a general change in attitude is needed to understand and cope with a fundamentally different environment.

The case is not meant to be a vehicle for exemplifying the ideas of any one particular motivational theorist. However, the case allows need and incentive theories (McClelland 1951; Maslow 1954; Herzberg 1959; Aldefer 1972; Dainty 1985) to be discussed and also the possibilities and difficulties of applying such frameworks to individual situations. Nevertheless, the case is meant to go further than considerations of which framework may or may not be applicable.

A number of motivational and development problems are generated within the case. These might be avoided, or at least reduced by a better understanding (stimulated by motivation frameworks) of the needs and weaknesses of the individuals involved in the case. Indeed, the first step in motivating or developing anyone must be an attempt to analyse these factors. But the case is meant to show that such an analysis is quite often not obvious, and the solutions are not straightforward. It isn't just a matter of identifying needs and then providing for these, as some need theories imply. Assessments of individuals will involve prejudice, misunderstanding, be clouded by image building, political behaviour, and by a lack of willingness by managers themselves to communicate their needs and problems. Sometimes they may not be fully aware of what their needs are.

Many of the issues in the case will have an impact on motivation in some way or another. These should be brought out during discussion, but the following points are of particular importance and should be highlighted.

1 Downward communication and sensitivity to issues.
2 Understanding of subordinates.
3 Organizational structure and development.
4 Political activity.
5 Personal development.

Downward communication and sensitivity to issues

Communication is particularly important in a contracting environment. To assume that saying nothing is a good policy during a period of change can cause greater problems within an organization, which may have both short- and long-term detrimental consequences. In the short term, if issues are not dealt with clearly then rumours will abound, not only causing some frustration, but possibly entrenching attitudes. In the long term, credible communication among the workforce may be much harder to achieve. In this case, the frustration and rumours that may occur are highlighted when Andrew meets administrative staff in a lift.

Even very difficult issues can be tackled if a company attempts to manage communication rather than be mismanaged by misunderstanding. For instance, there may be no easily accepted substitute for the reduction of material rewards, such as pay. However, these may be acccpted if communicated thoughtfully, again as highlighted in the case. Their reduction consequently may not greatly affect motivation especially if everyone suffers equally. Even so, the reduction or removal of even minor perks can be explosive if handled badly. In this case, Larry shows some insensitivity to how changes in incentives and status may be received generally (free managers' lunches and separate dining hall facilities).

Understanding of subordinates

As noted earlier, individuals cannot begin to be motivated unless there is some understanding by their managers of them as individuals. This is too easily forgotten or blinded by other aspects, such as lack of time, infrequency of contact, misinformed comments of others, and our own assumptions and values, etc. The consequences, may, in the long term, have severe problems for a company leading to demotivation (possibly for John in the future) and resignation (possibly for Andrew). In this case, Larry shows a lack of understanding of the needs and motivation of his staff. Unconcerned about the problems of some (John) he is also blind to the frustrations and problems of others (Andrew and Tony). Ted also shows a lack of understanding of the frustrations of younger managers (Andrew), of understanding how to help older managers adapt (Tony), and in helping other managers with remedial problems and with coping strategies (John).

Organizational structure and development

Concern with maintaining the managerial structure of a company may mask or sidetrack managers from considering other important issues. Ted exemplifies concern with maintaining the management structure, which overrides assessments of managerial needs, abilities and weaknesses. This concern may be detrimental in the long term. Restricted promotion opportunities affect both motivation and management development. While promotion may be severely restricted, this should not result in removing managers' aspirations, but in rethinking how limited opportunities are used both in terms of who is promoted and how this is communicated.

In this case, Andrew represents the younger, qualified and mobile member of staff. He is ambitious and wishes to broaden his skills and abilities. At the moment he does not have a motivational problem, and would still seem to be largely committed to the organization. A number of things are frustrating him, however, and ensuing events are likely to affect him considerably. Keen to get ahead, his immediate promotion opportunities and chances of a lateral transfer are now blocked by people he regards as less competent than himself. His most likely response is to leave the company which does not seem to be able to fully accommodate his needs, reduce his increasing frustration, or hold much of a future for him. If he stays, additional factors, such as the reduction in 'perks' are likely to add to his frustrations, possibly reduce his motivation and increase his antagonism towards the company.

Tony exemplifies the promotional blockage. The most important problem in terms of motivation may be his impact on other staff. His appearance of not being fully up to his job, lack of promotion potential and complacency, affect both Andrew and John, (and will have a greater impact after John's demotion). The image that Larry has of him bringing stability to the company is not shared by his staff.

Political activity

The possibility of greater political activity within a company may leave 'complacent' managers vulnerable. The need, at least, to be aware of political behaviour is particularly important. One may find that in a contracting environment, the rules of the game one is used to may no longer apply. But by the time one has come to terms with that, one may no longer be in the game. Any attempt to understand and come to terms with changing organizational patterns of behaviour can only enhance an individual's position in difficult circumstances.

On the one hand Tony represents the manager who may operate politically well and survive as a result, but who may be difficult to motivate and to make more effective. A long time in the company, he has enough experience to ensure his position and maintain his security. Despite some awareness of 'problems' by senior staff, he seems to be 'well in' enough for these to be ignored. However, he is unlikely to respond either to the positive or negative incentives that a company normally offers.

On the other hand, John is the solid worker who has not come to terms with the changed environment especially in political terms. His concern is more with feeling secure than getting ahead. Motivated by doing a good day's work in his terms and being appreciated, he would seem to lack realistic feedback. However, he highlights the need for individuals to develop new personal strategies for survival, and the need to engage in a minimum of political activity such as image building. Also important is the need for John to increase his own marketability not only internally but also outside the company.

Personal development

The changing environment will bring a number of additional work problems. Clearly, these problems will vary between companies, between functions and between managers. There is a need for managers to receive formal training or instruction, especially, for instance, in understanding ways of coping with pressure, and with stress, managing time effectively, etc. All the managers in the case highlight this aspect. However, often problems may be exacerbated if managers feel they cannot share problems, and especially if the problems faced are new ones, without solutions in a journal or textbook. The provision of non threatening, but structured problem solving/discussion meetings for managers with similar problems, and/or in similar functions, possibly even from other companies, could be a particularly useful learning forum. John highlights the need to provide for himself, or have provided, opportunities to discuss issues and overcome problems along these lines.

Additionally, there may be a particular need for changes in managerial attitude. For instance, in this case, Ted represents the management development adviser who has not come to terms with looking at new ways of development, of selling the importance of management development in such an environment and making it relevant. While Tony highlights the major problem of how to change a manager's antagonistic/sceptical attitude towards development and admitting weakness. He may need a major jolt if he is to accept the relevance of new behaviours to improve his effectiveness. But in a situation of scarce resources, the burden may be much more on the individual to take responsibility for his/her own development and also for communicating his/her needs and frustrations, rather than expect other members of the organization to find out what they might be, or do it accurately. Again, if there is any 'answer' to the case it is the acceptance that the environment is not a total straitjacket and that both at an organizational and a personal level the need to develop coping strategies is essential.

Teaching guide summary

Issues	*Learning points*
1 Downward communication.	• Bad communication has short- and long-term consequences.
	• Manage communication.
	• Keep workforce informed.
	• Actively try to reduce rumours.
	• Even small items handled badly can have a major impact.
	• Sensitivity to the issues.
2 Understanding of subordinates.	• Easy to say.
	• But often understanding is poor due to: lack of time infrequency of contact misinformed comments own values and assumptions.
	• Misunderstanding may lead to: demotivation lack of commitment
3 Organizational structure and development.	• Maintaining structure may: not maintain stability prevent staff development prevent most effective use of resources have long-term consequences reduce motivation mean loss of mobile staff.

4	Political activity.	• May increase in a situation of scarce resources.
		• May leave complacent managers vulnerable.
		• Need to be aware of politics.
		• Need to be aware of changing rules.
		• Image building.
5	Personal development.	• Changing work problems.
		• Need to cope with more pressure.
		• Need for discussion opportunities.
		• Need to review at work methods.
		• Need to review at attitudes.
		• Need to consider ways of communicating needs/frustrations.
		• Personal responsibility for development.
		• Develop new coping strategies overall.

Teaching style

The case may either be tackled individually or in groups. Individually the audience should be asked to read the case and answer the questions at the end. If a group approach is used then split the audience into groups of six or seven. Ask the groups to discuss the questions at the end of the case. Make available enough flipcharts/acetates/whiteboards in order that the groups may present their findings. If the case is answered individually, then two or three members of the audience should be asked to present their conclusions.

After the groups or individuals have made their presentations then identify the five learning points outlined earlier. These should then be used in conjunction with the issues raised by each group directly in relation to motivation and management development, to get a comprehensive picture of the issues in the case. The major point to conclude the case on is the need for personal awareness and coping strategies in a changed and often harsh environment.

References

C. P. Aldefer, *Existence, Relatedness and Growth. Human Needs in Organizational Settings*, (Free Press, New York, 1972).

P. H. Dainty, 'How to Manage Retreat', *Management Today*, (November 1985).

F. Herzberg, B. Mausner and B. Snyderman, *The Motivation to Work*, (Wiley, New York, 1959).

A. H. Maslow, *Motivation and Personality*, (Harper, New York, 1954).

D. C. McClelland, *Personality*, (Dryden Press, New York, 1951).

THREE

Kleine Plastics

RON LUDLOW

Part 2

When David walked into the boardroom at 9.00 a.m. on Monday morning, he was surprised to find there was nobody else there. However, within ten minutes the other managers had arrived, with the exception of Ian Breed. Each offered his apologies for being late, but explained that the meeting had been called at very short notice and they all had outstanding business to attend to, which they could not put off. Ian Breed arrived at 9.20 a.m. He politely, but firmly, told David that Monday morning was the busiest morning of the week, involving the scheduling of production for the entire week. There could not have been a more awkward time to hold a meeting.

David calmly accepted their apologies but emphasized that this was an urgent meeting. He had studied the cost, sales and production figures and was not impressed by what he had seen. He felt that the production costs were far too high and he told the meeting that his first objective, as acting Managing Director, was to bring these down.

First, he addressed Bob Spender, the purchasing manager. He pointed out that the purchase price of raw materials seemed high and queried the heavy use of a single supplier. Bob said that the company had used this supplier for many years and although his prices were not the cheapest, the materials were of the highest quality. David instructed him to carry out a full raw materials review, to get quotes from several other suppliers and not to reorder until they had discussed the matter further.

He then turned to Victor Keane, pointing out that the high cost of production was not solely dependent on the purchase price of raw materials alone. He believed that the sales forecasts were too low

17

and, after giving a curt explanation of fixed and variable costs, concluded: 'Sell more and the price will come down'. Victor Keane was swift to defend his sales projections and also the dynamism of his sales team. David then suggested that perhaps sales could be boosted by extending the colour range of their products. Victor replied that there did not appear to be any dissatisfaction among buyers with their present range of colours. David was determined to press the point and asked Victor whether he had ever considered commissioning a market survey. Finding the reply to be negative, David announced that he had decided to do this immediately. Moreover, he had been thinking about the potential for the new water tank and believed that sales could be raised if they marketed it as a domestic oil-storage tank, as well as a water tank. This could make it highly attractive to the UK and European markets. He therefore proposed contacting an ex-college friend, who was now a marketing consultant, and commissioning him to carry out the market survey for existing products and also to advise on marketing the new water tank.

At this point, Ian Breed pointed out that extending the colour range would involve his department in extensive rescheduling and added that, in his opinion, a wider range of colour would not necessarily mean the production of more items. He considered that production was at its peak, that they could not produce more with the present machinery and manpower. He also reminded David that the water tank production was still in its test-run stage, and added that they were experiencing some problems. The tanks were sticking to the moulds and the finished items were not getting through quality control.

David rounded on him, sharply pointing out that he was not satisfied with the present production schedules. He felt that it was time the company called in a time and motion expert. He was convinced that production could be increased and that the colour range could be extended, without having to increase either the manpower or machinery capacity. With regard to the problems of the water tank production, he suggested that they had better sort them out quickly, as they had promised to deliver the first batch by the end of the month. The meeting ended abruptly as David stood up, gathered up his papers and walked to the door. At the door, he turned. 'Thank you, gentlemen. You have plenty to get on with,' was all he said, as he quickly left the room.

As David walked back to his office, Alan Foulkes caught up with him. Alan expressed concern over David's somewhat dictatorial attitude. He suggested that David might adopt a more consultative approach when dealing with the managers and pointed out their vast experience. He also gently reminded him of his father's method of dealing with them. Before he could go any further, David stopped, turned to him and said, 'When I need your advice, I will ask for it.' With this, he walked on, leaving Alan Foulkes open-mouthed.

David returned to his office, convinced that his positive attitude was the right one to adopt. He felt that the company could do with shaking up and that his dynamic approach would result in increased production and greater profitability.

Questions

1   Are the senior managers likely to/not to/work together to improve the position? Why?
2   Is David's leadership style likely to be effective/not effective? Why?
3   Will morale on the shop floor increase/decrease? Why?

Part 3

Having commissioned the marketing consultant and appointed a time and motion expert to start work the following Monday, David devoted the rest of the week to trying to solve the problems of the sticking water tanks. He sent a memo to the chief designer, Charles Penfold, asking him to come to his office for a discussion on Friday afternoon. At this meeting, he explained that he believed that some of the problem could be caused by faults in the initial design and asked for Charles's comments. Needless to say, Charles defended his design, saying that if the mould was sticking it was nothing to do with the basic design and that the fault must lie with the Production Department. He suggested that David should find out whether or not they applied a sealing agent to the mould before they injected the plastic material. David immediately sent a memo to Ian Breed, raising this query.

The following Monday morning, he was greeted by his secretary, who told him that Ian Breed had phoned and that he was very angry. Apparently, Ian had been completely unaware that the time and motion expert would be in the factory that morning. David had said nothing further to Ian about this matter, since the meeting the previous Monday. He immediately sent for Ian and, after a brief apology for his oversight, asked him about the use of a sealant. Ian replied that it was not the usual practice to use a sealant on a new mould and that, in any case, the company did not possess a heavy-duty sealant suitable for this particular mould. When he had left, David immediately sent a memo to purchasing, telling them to order the appropriate sealant. He then sent a memo to Ian Breed, telling him to stop all test runs on the water tank until the sealant had been applied to the mould.

Before the sealant arrived, David decided to break with the usual production procedures with regard to the new water tank. He sent for Ian Breed and told him that he intended to set up a separate team for this job. The report from the marketing consultant confirmed that there was indeed a potential market for the tank in domestic oil-storage and so he intended giving top priority to its production. He had therefore decided to appoint a production engineer from outside the company, to head this team, who would have overall charge of its production on a daily basis.

He sent a memo to Victor Keane, informing him to instruct his sales team to give top priority to the development of the market for the new tank, both in the UK and in Europe. However, he pointed out that there were no plans to increase the sales force. He also advised Victor that the marketing consultant had reported a market potential for extending the colour range of their plasticware, and that he wanted brochures prepared accordingly.

In early January, the time and motion expert reported that some improvements could be made which would increase productivity, but, in order to extend the colour range, new machinery and more staff would be needed. The existing manpower and machinery capacity would only achieve replacement sales.

Bob Spender informed David that he had finished the raw materials review, and David asked him to come to his office immediately for a discussion. David was delighted with Bob's work. He had prepared a twenty-page report which listed all the suppliers of raw plastic, together with details of prices and delivery. He advised David that he had contacted the company which offered the lowest price, and that they had enough raw material to fill Kleine's order. Delivery would take three days. He also confirmed that the sealant for the water tank mould had arrived. David was very pleased. He authorized the raw material order straight away, and congratulated Bob on his success, inviting him to have a drink with him at lunchtime.

At the end of January, David decided to stop the manufacture of the company's range of plasticware in red, and replace it with cerise, a colour shown to be in demand by the recent market survey. He promptly advised Ian Breed, who told him that he had been instructed to run red by the Sales Department, in order to fill outstanding orders. David insisted that he proceed with cerise, and instructed sales to inform all customers that Kleine had stopped making red plasticware and instead was now filling their orders with the current fashion colour, cerise. Three weeks later, the warehouse manager reported that he had a storage problem. Stocks of the new cerise plasticware were building up and he had nowhere to store them. When David raised this matter with Victor Keane, he was told that sales had not been given enough time to introduce the new colour to customers.

Questions

1 Are the senior managers likely/unlikely to work together to improve the position? Why?
2 Is David's leadership style effective/not effective? Why?
3 Will morale on the shop floor increase/decrease? Why?

Part 4

On the factory floor, morale declined. The moulders complained that the raw material from the new supplier was difficult to work with. Quality control rejected more finished items, because they were below the accepted standard. Ian Breed had tried to increase the production rate, in accordance with David's instructions, but had met with resistance. The senior shop steward had warned him that health and safety standards would be jeopardized. In any case, with the present problems over the raw material, it was proving hard enough to maintain the production level, yet alone increase it. David refused to accept any of these excuses, and accused Ian Breed of being awkward. From then on, all contact between them was limited to memoranda.

The team producing the water tank at last started a production run, but the initial problems resulted in production being over six weeks behind schedule. Sales secured a few orders for the tanks to be used in domestic oil storage, both in the UK and Europe, but the delay in production caused some cancellations.

Behind his closed office door, David was busy sketching a design for plastic garden furniture, which he intended asking the design team to develop. He was interrupted by the telephone ringing. The local garage informed him that the Mercedes he had ordered three weeks ago had arrived, and would be delivered before the end of the day.

At the end of February, Joseph returned. He was greeted by a storm of complaints from all the managers. Having heard and digested their stories of what went on during his absence, he returned to his office, his face red and the veins standing out on his temples and neck. His eyes blazed with anger, as he caught sight of a large Mercedes driving into a space marked 'Reserved for Directors'.

Questions

1   What action, if any, will Joseph Kleine take to change the situation?

Introduction

The case of Kleine Plastics examines the differences between two contrasting styles of management at senior management level. It can be used to highlight key aspects of management style, and to show the importance of interpersonal skills which are necessary at any level by managers in an organization.

Theory and background

The case examines the style differences between the 'person orientated' manager and the 'production orientated' manager. It highlights the necessity of being aware of what the consequences of behaving in these two differing management styles are likely to be in an organization which has become familiar with and whose culture has been built upon one particular management style. It highlights the difficulties of trying to change an organizational culture by imposition rather than by pursuasion, education, consultation, participation, and involvement. It illustrates that where these elements are absent in the change process, no effective change is likely to occur, and resistance to change is likely to increase, causing frustration and interpersonal stress within the organization.

Key learning points

The case illustrates the differences in management style of Joseph Kleine, the founder of Kleine Plastics, and that of his son, David. In particular the following points during case discussion should be drawn to the students' attention:

1 Characteristics and consequences of 'person orientated' management.
2 Characteristics and consequences of 'production orientated' management.
3 The use of situational leadership.

Characteristics and consequences of 'person orientated' management

Joseph Kleine is actively involved in the day-to-day management of his company. He makes a point of 'touring' the works twice a day. In this way, he knows exactly what is going on, can deal with any trouble before it really develops and by talking to his managers at their work stations he does not divert them from their jobs.

This practice shows the workers the 'visible' face of management. Joseph uses this opportunity to motivate his staff while keeping his ear to the ground.

He is patriarchal, a benevolent despot, yet dynamic and charismatic, with sound technical knowledge. His managers enjoy a fair degree of autonomy – because Joseph trusts their ability and is willing to delegate. He sees himself in a supporting role, always there to lend assistance should the managers require it. Mutual technical and personal respect exist between Joseph and his managers.

A plain speaker, he is quick to chastise and equally quick to praise. He is not a 'political animal,' power-play is not his game. 'Politics is for Westminster' is one of his favourite sayings, and he deals with disagreements between managers fairly and equitably.

He is also a charismatic leader, with whom his managers and his work force wish to identify. He sees relationships as two-way; he trusts and respects his managers and employees, and understands their problems, while on the other hand they give him their trust and respect and commitment to high task performance. He sees his organization's major assets to be the people who work there; without them there would be no organization.

Characteristics and consequences of 'production orientated' management

David Kleine is not at all like his father. Not for him the 'tour' of the works, but instead he sits behind his desk and communicates by telephone and memo. When he needs to see a manager, he calls him into his office. It is as if he is playing the role of manager, as he sees it, and he sees it as not getting involved with people and personalities, but concentrating on task achievement.

David Kleine represents the 'invisible' face of management to the workers. His sole contact is with the managers.

While he has inherited his father's dynamism, unfortunately for

Kleine Plastics his dynamism is not tempered by diplomacy. David wants to be in the driving seat to such an extent that he erodes the working autonomy of his managers. He risks demotivating them and causing a decline in morale. He is also likely to spread dissension among them.

Like his father he is also quick to chastise and to praise, but in his case, 'power-play' is the name of game. He praises and rewards those who cooperate with him without question. Therefore, the purchasing manager who produces the raw materials review and locates a supply of cheaper material, is rewarded with verbal praise and a lunchtime drink – technical and social acknowledgement.

On the other hand, the other managers suffer harassment and pressure – none more so than the production manager, Ian Breed. First, his production schedule is criticized. David wants more items produced and in a wider colour range. He ignores Ian's protestations over the inadequacy of the manpower and machinery, and calls in a time and motion expert. This questions Ian Breed's experience and knowledge of the resources under his control, striking at the core of his technical ability, and his power base within the organization.

David later compounds this when he takes the production of the new water tank away from Ian's control, by setting up a separate section to be managed by a production engineer brought in from outside the company. When Ian experiences serious problems in increasing the production rate, both from a health and safety aspect and because of the difficulties caused by the cheaper raw materials, David refuses to listen. He interprets Ian's arguments as being 'excuses' and accuses him of being 'awkward'. Communication between the two becomes non-existent. Contact is only by memo. The morale on the factory floor declines.

David's poor interpersonal skills result in increasing chaos for the company. His interference with the production run, when he orders cerise to be substituted for red, results in a stockpile of the new coloured items, which causes storage problems in the warehouse. The sales team complain they have not had enough time to introduce the colour change to their customers, hence the stockpile.

The sales team get orders for the water tank (to be used in domestic oil storage), which cannot be filled because of production problems. This also results in loss of orders.

David never consults his managers. He takes independent decisions in each discipline, without thinking how they could interrelate and do interact. In three months he erodes the established system of managerial autonomy which his father has built up. In its place he establishes his own managerial control system.

He is obsessed with statistics, and is quite convinced that he knows how to increase sales and raise the profitability of the company. He completely ignores the fact that he was not given a mandate for either action, but that it was meant to perform a 'holding' operation only, during his father's absence.

He has seen it as his chance to prove himself. It is unlikely that he has succeeded.

The use of situational leadership

Kleine Plastics is a small company in the process of growing and developing. It has many of the characteristics of a typical small company, for example a charismatic leader, close personal relationships between the managers themselves and the managers and their workforce, the ability to react quickly to change, and to perceive opportunities, personal contact between managers and workers at all levels, and an atmosphere of trust and openness based on mutual respect for technical and interpersonal competence etc. Both its managers and its workforce were at an average to high stage of development with respect to the activities they had to perform and the tasks they had to achieve. In such a situation the participatory and delegative managerial style of Joseph Kleine was appropriate. The level of risk he took with respect to the autonomy granted to managers and workers was commensurate with his perception of the limits of their abilities and competence with respect to these tasks. He was, by nature and personality, a people-centred person who wished to involve people in participation and decision-making. As he said himself, 'without people there is no organization'.

On the other hand, David Kleine's managerial style is that of directing and controlling and setting up complex management information systems to enable him to make decisions by himself without consultation with other managers. This style of direction and control, instead of participating and consulting, is more appropriate where managers and the workforce are at a low stage of ability and motivation with respect to the tasks they are required to perform. Little wonder that frustration and resentment built up against this style of management which was not characteristic of the culture and climate of Kleine Plastics which had evolved over the past twenty years.

David Kleine also suffered from a lack of effective interpersonal skills, in relation to those perceived in his father. In this small organization, the fabric of openness and trust was being torn apart by David's remote and formal style of communication. In any leadership situation, effective interpersonal communication is critical for success.

Teaching guide summary

Issues	*Learning points*

1 Person orientated management.	• Personal style preferences.
	• Personal power:
	    expert (technical competence)
	    referent power (charisma).
	• Concern for people.
	• Relationship-building.
	• Interpersonal communication.
	• Mutual trust and respect.
	• Monitoring systems.
	• 'Visible' management.
	• Participation and consultation.

2 Production orientated management.	• Personal style preferences.
	• Individual values and objectives.
	• Concern for task achievement.
	• Belief in rationality and logical analysis.
	• Use of position power:
	    coercive
	    reward
	    connection

3 Span of control.	• Formal and remote communication. • Interpersonal skills. • Lack of trust. • Personal goals. • Lack of insight and understanding of people.

4 Situational leadership.	• Task/and person/orientation.
	• Personal values and preferred styles.
	• Job related ability and motivation of subordinates.
	• Skills required for effective situational leadership:
	    diagnostic skills
	    skills in flexing managerial style
	    effective communication
	    effect of existing organisational culture.

Teaching style

Make available white boards/black boards, or flip charts to the groups.

Ask the groups to present the results of their discussion of each question. Write on the boards the key findings of each group. After the groups have finished their presentations, fit their findings into the structure of the teaching guide on a separate board. As the key points emerge, relate this to situational leadership theory, and ask them to relate situational leadership theory to their own job and work environments.

In the closing summary of the case, highlight the importance of interpersonal skills as a key factor in effective managers, and the diagnostic and style-flexibility skills which are necessary for them to use effectively situational leadership in their own work.

FOUR

Henry Smart

RON LUDLOW

Introduction

The case of Henry Smart examines interpersonal perceptions; particularly the different perceptions of the same person by different people, and why their perceptions differ.

Theory and background

Interpersonal perception is the process whereby external stimulae are translated into terms which are relevant to and have meaning to the receiver (the perceiver). People constantly respond to cues which have meaning for them and them alone. They see what they want, or need to see. They do not see (perceive) other people as they are: they see them for what they mean to themselves. So two people may receive the same visual and oral stimulae, but have completely different perceptions of them, and what they mean.

People, in fact, have their own personal frames of reference, affected by their personal attitudes, prejudices, backgrounds, and experiences which provide standards against which other persons' actions and behaviours are judged and evaluated. This results in individuals having a distorted view of the real world 'out there', a subjective view of reality which can only be made more objective in real terms by they themselves generating a higher sense of self awareness, a greater understanding of their own self-concept. One method of achieving this greater understanding by the processes of self-disclosure and feedback from other people.

People develop their own sets of concepts that they use to interpret other peoples' behaviour. They aggregate these sets of concepts together to form a conceptual system which they use to form images of other people in order to predict their behaviour. Information from and about other people tends to come in small, discrete bits. The individual, using his frame of reference, his own conceptual system, takes in these small bits of information and from them draws implications with respect to other characteristics of the other person. This of course leads to perceptual biases which affect mutual understanding and relationships between people in organizations.

Key learning points

The case concentrates on the interpersonal relationships between individuals in the firm of Smart & Company and the effects of interpersonal perception upon those relationships. In particularly the following points during case discussion, need to be drawn to the students' attention:

1 Causes of interpersonal perception.
2 Consequences of interpersonal perception.
3 Managing interpersonal perception.

Causes of interpersonal perception

Let us consider the three major characters in this case, Henry Smart, Alec Smart and Marilyn, and how their frames of reference, their conceptual systems, have evolved.

Henry Smart

Henry Smart was the son of the firm's founder, and a partner since 1946. He perceived himself to be the 'manager' – his partner, John Newbold, deals only with financial matters. He sees himself as being dynamic and aggressive in business terms – it is his idea to expand operations into the 'commercial' market. He is childless and paternalistic, he sees the firm as his 'family'. He values loyalty and ability, particularly in his staff. He has concern for people, and has good interpersonal skills – seeing mutual respect as the key to success.

Alec Smart

Alec Smart is a dynamic negotiator, used to the 'cut and thrust' of London. He is a good social mixer, unmarried and ambitious: not a 'nine to five' person. He knows that his way of working is right for 'commercial' work. He values autonomy; and his autonomous way of working pays off financially for the organization (the firm's profits have increased due to his method of working). He is very aware of his 'inheritance' prospects – both privately and commercially.

Marilyn
Marilyn is the office administrator: she sees herself as the champion of the 'established system' – this system she sees as an extension of her own ego. She perceives that it is her job to receive and delegate the work from the negotiators, and any disruption of the system is a threat to her system and her personally.

Let us consider now the interpersonal perceptions existing between these characters in Smart & Company.

1 *Henry Smart* perceives *Alec Smart* as possessing some disturbing qualities, for example, he is unable to temper his aggression within the office; he is an isolationist; he has alienated the other staff; he has appropriated the services of the junior. However, he likes Alec Smart (he sees much of himself in him); he acknowledges Alec's input into the firm's profitability; he knows that he is popular with clients; he perceives him to have ability and drive – clients like his efficiency; he realizes that enforced adherence to the 'office system' might demotivate and frustrate Alec.

There are certain implications and questions raised by Henry's perception of Alec.

Does Henry see Alec as a threat – the young buck and the old stag? If Alec is made a partner, what effect will that have on Henry's position?
Which way would John Newbold go then – towards Henry or Alec?
Is part of the dilemma the conflict of Henry's values and beliefs as a manager versus his values and beliefs as a negotiator?

2 *Marilyn* sees *Alec Smart* as using bypassing manoeuvres, which threaten the existing system, and thus threaten her status and self-concept. She perceives him to be the indirect cause of her being reprimanded by the other negotiators; a selfish, thoughtless young man, who causes stress to the typists by his insistence that his work should have 'priority' when he arrives back late in the office. He causes dissension among the other negotiators. However, she perceives him as being genuinely appreciative of the typists' cooperation in his work (he buys them chocolates). She perceives that he has ability which makes him potential partnership material,

but she would be against this, until he can accept, and work within, the system.

3 *Alec Smart* sees *Henry Smart* as a childless uncle, who offered him the chance to set up and run the new Commercial Department, and who might well make him his heir. Henry controls Alec's short- and long-term prospects. He sees Henry as being rather stuffy, pompous, and paternalistic and feels that Henry is constraining his opportunities to work effectively. He feels that Henry does not really understand Alec's special needs for flexibility within the system to make the new Commercial Department work well and grow and develop.

Alec sees *Marilyn* as the slave of the system and that the system is wrong for 'commercial' work. However, the typists do not mind his direct approach; they work for him willingly and efficiently.

Alec Smart perceives the *other negotiators* as jealous of his success. They are reactive, slow, not dynamic – they wait for business to come to them, rather than looking for business by themselves. They do not train their staff properly or adequately. However, he also perceives that this jealousy of him could be a force for good – a catalyst for their self improvement.

Consequences of interpersonal perception

To Marilyn, Alec should be part of the system. She dislikes him because he is not stopped. The established system is Marilyn's 'comfort zone' – Alec is violating it.

Henry takes the broader view. He sees Alec from a frame of reference both inside and outside the office system. He recognizes Alec's ability and drive, which have resulted in a substantial contribution to the firm's profits. Yet, he also recognizes that his nephew is a potential liability. By keeping Alec in the firm with a long-term view to partnership, Henry could risk the short-term disaffection and demotivation of the rest of his staff. They all adhere to the system. Alec does not.

Henry's dilemma is how to marry the man to the system, without inducing in him a loss of drive and innovation.

Alec has drive and ambition. He is dramatically successful, increasing the firm's turnover by 25 per cent in the first six months' of his employment. He sees the Commercial Department as being different from the domestic property market, in that it takes more energy and 'pushiness' to get business.

He thinks and acts as though he is working for a separate operation. The system which Marilyn guards so fiercely is not the right one for commercial work. His direct approach to the typists works. The established custom and practice by which the other negotiators work is interpreted by Alec as being 'slow', lacking drive and aggression. He believes that their complaints are founded on jealousy.

Alec has a very strong self-concept, at no time does he express any self-doubt. He is a 'workaholic' who judges his fellow negotiators by his standards. He clearly has no respect for them, even denouncing their training of the junior as 'inadequate'. He therefore feels no compunction in taking over the junior without referring to those in charge of training.

Note his response to Henry's reprimand. At no time does he admit any fault on his part. Yet, at the end of their conversation, although he appears mollified, he makes no statement about, or gives any commitment with respect to, his future conduct. In fact, it is Alec who brings the meeting to an abrupt end by reminding Henry that he is keeping a client waiting, demonstrating that he puts client goodwill before anything else.

His subsequent behaviour could well be seen as a 'sop' to placate Henry. On the other hand, it could be that of a square peg trying to fit into a round hole – and failing. The verdict on Alec could be either a man who will not fit the system, or one who cannot fit the system.

As a consequence of these interpersonal perceptions, certain dangers and threats to individual self-concepts can be identified.

To *Henry Smart* the threat is twofold; Alec Smart does not conform – this is a threat to the system which, with Marilyn, he was instrumental in setting up. Alec is also a potential threat to Henry's image as the dynamic driving force behind Smart & Company because of Alec's unprecedented success in setting up and developing the Commercial Department.

Marilyn is threatened because Alec disrupts and pressurizes her. She identifies with the system, and any threat to that is a threat to her self-concept.

Alec is threatened because of Henry's remonstrations; but perhaps he does not see this as an attack, as he does not modify his behaviour. He makes a gesture of conformity only for a temporary period.

Alec Smart is also threatened by Marilyn, as guardian of the system. He feels that unwarranted barriers are being placed before him by her, and the system, particularly as he is making such a valuable contribution to the profitability of the firm.

Teaching guide summary

Issues	*Learning points*
1 Interpersonal perception.	• What is perception? selecting and organizing external sensory stimulae and information into terms and categories which are meaningful and consistent with our own frames of reference • Influences on perception: limited information self-disclosure feedback from other people attributes factors in the situation perceptual biases in the perceiver/and the perceived. • Internal states. • External situations. • Noise in the system. • Frames of reference. • Conceptual systems.
2 Consequences of interpersonal perception.	• Rejection of non-congruent cues. • Selective perception. • Interpersonal conflict. values beliefs goals influence expectancies of outcomes of actions. • Self-fulfilling prophecy. • Forming false images of others. • Threats to individual self-concepts.
3 Managing the perception process.	• Developing a high sense of self-awareness. • Strong self-concept. • Self-disclosure and feedback from other people.

- Not forming hasty judgements on limited information.
- Not assuming consistent behaviour in different situations.
- Active listening.
- Role perception.

Teaching style

Make available white boards/black boards and flip charts for each group where possible.

Ask the groups to present the results of their discussion of each question. Summarize on the white board/black board the key findings of each group. Fit these findings into the structure of the teaching guide on a separate board. Particularly consider with the class what actions Henry Smart could take to improve this situation, and what the likely consequences are if no action is taken. Encourage discussion with the class, exploring whether they recognize these key points in the case and can relate them back into their own work environment. Ask them to give examples of problems caused by errors in perception in their work environment.

In the closing summary of the case, highlight the importance of testing out various perceptions of people and situations before coming to any judgements or making any decisions. Emphasize that for perceptions to be free of bias, it is necessary to have a strong self-concept and to actively work at building up rapport, mutual respect and trust with other people to ensure the development of effective interpersonal communication and relationships. Particularly emphasize the need to have a high sense of self-awareness, i.e. 'Physician, heal thyself!'

FIVE AND SIX

Peter Johnson and Maurice Bradley

DAVID BUTCHER AND CATHERINE BAILEY

Appendix 1 Peter Johnson

Subject: Peter Johnson, Envelope factory manager

Premier Manufacturing and Supplies is a major manufacturer of stationery and office accessories. Traditionally it has had a stable market share although more recently the market has become more competitive and the company has come under pressure to define its marketing strategy more closely. Premier has a skilled workforce and a low labour turnover. It is the largest employer in the area and many employees spend their entire working lives with the company.

You are thirty-seven years of age and have been with Premier one year as envelope factory manager. Prior to this your entire career had been spent with Trident Aviation Ltd from where you were made redundant last year. You were not keen to be applying for jobs from a position of unemployment and so cast your net wide. The Premier job was the first good offer which came your way and you took it without too much deliberation, thereby avoiding any break in employment.

As envelope factory manager you have full responsibility for managing all aspects of the unit and you report directly to Ken Firth, Production Director. Your three production line supervisors have all been with the company several years and are all competent in their jobs. You are happy in general with the way you have been tackling the job and you consider it something of an achievement that in the space of one year production rates on all three of your product lines are up, wastage rates have dropped, morale in the factory is higher, safety procedures are being better observed and there has been an overall tightening up on house-keeping. Indeed all of this has been achieved in the face of what in your view is a rather antiquated approach to management in the company generally. Compared with the dynamism of the aviation industry with which you are so familiar the Premier culture has an old fashioned benevolent paternalism about it. You find this frustrating, in fact recently you confided as much to a colleague on the departmental management team, Mark Old, the quality control manager. The monthly departmental management team meetings are a good example of this low key approach to management. Ken Firth is not a good Chairman and the meetings go on far too long – half a day sometimes. This is half a day you could be spending on operational matters in the factory which require your attention. The management team's approach to problems seems to be to give them a good airing and then agree to keep a watching brief on them. In your view the team is merely a forum for discussion whereas it should have some clear decision making role if it is going to be effective. Ken also encourages the factory managers to air detailed production problems. Usually you feel the answers are fairly obvious and anyway management team is not the place to be discussing them.

In contrast to your impact in management team meetings you feel you have at least been able to create a greater business awareness in the envelope factory. This you have achieved in a number of ways. First, you have made considerable efforts to communicate directly with the shop floor and you have also set up small discussion groups which meet to consider ways of improving effectiveness in the factory. These appear to have generated a lot of enthusiasm and some good ideas – more than you had expected. Second to minimize bureaucracy impeding efficiency you try to keep communication informal and to avoid nit-picking. For example, one of your supervisors, Barry Walsh, recently claimed 450 miles for a trip that ought to be about 300 miles return, when using a pool car to visit a raw materials supplier in Middlesbrough. You happen to know from one of his chargehands that Barry took the opportunity to visit his mother in Newcastle, staying overnight with her, which accounted for the extra 150 miles claimed. However, he did not claim overnight expenses which in your mind reasonably offset the extra travelling expenses incurred. Technically you know you should have taken it up with him but it hardly seemed to justify the irritation this might cause, particularly as Barry had managed to sort out a long-standing difficulty with that particular supplier. You therefore said nothing and authorized his claim. One other way you have tried to foster business awareness in the factory is by creating team spirit. You feel that your staff are now quite proud of the factory and its record over the past few months. It has particularly worried you, therefore, when Nigel Davies and Mike Hollows, the other factory managers, have asked to borrow some of your office staff when they have been under pressure. You agreed on each occasion but you do not like the factory 'team' to be disrupted for extended periods in this way. Similarly you are not happy about the personnel job evaluation exercise being carried out in each factory. Job evaluation in your experience usually leads to disruption and dissatisfaction, and you feel this exercise is likely to undo a lot of what you have achieved in building up the morale of your staff. You have had several awkward discussions with the Director of Personnel on the subject of the job evaluation exercise, and you are aware he feels you are being uncooperative by not making your staff available for interview by personnel. While you do not feel well disposed towards making your staff available, the fact is that it is very difficult to fit these interviews into the production schedules.

One thing that you would like to bring up with Ken Firth at your forthcoming appraisal interview is his weekly visits to the factory. Ken managed the envelope factory until he became Director of Production four years ago and knows many of the employees well. You feel he often keeps individuals talking too long as he does his round, which he does unaccompanied by you, and you also wonder whether some of the older employees may relate to Ken rather than you, in which case his tours probably don't help this situation.

You are a little worried that Ken may want to talk about your growing involvement with the Marketing Department. Over the past couple of months you have had several discussions with the Director of Marketing, initiated in the first place by him, but more recently you have sought his views on some restructuring of the factory which you have in mind. He does seem to have a refreshingly business-like approach to managing Premier and his ideas about restructuring your unit to give greater capacity to the special project line, thus allowing more flexibility in producing special order, high quality batches, make a lot of sense given the current market demands. These ideas are reflected in a paper on restructuring the envelope factory which you gave to Ken Firth last week. However, you know Ken and the Director of Marketing do not see eye to eye, although you are not altogether sure why, and you wonder whether Ken may take a jaundiced view of the report and whether he feels undermined by your liaison with the Director of Marketing.

You are waiting outside Ken's office for your appraisal interview, the first you have had since joining Premier. . . .

Appendix 2 Maurice Bradley

Subject: Maurice Bradley, Maintenance section head

You have been with Wessex and in post for one year and are happy by and large at the way things are going. You are proud of the fact that during this time you have managed to raise the motivation and performance of your section considerably, particularly so because having been refused your request by Personnel for an additional assistant engineer shortly after your arrival you made a conscious decision to try to develop the effectiveness of your staff to meet the section's increasing workload. You feel you have a good relationship with your staff and your young assistant engineers seem keen to get on.

Your main responsibilities are to identify and programme any maintenance work required, respond to emergency work required, organizing the letting of contracts and if the direct labour section is involved, to brief Dennis Marshall, the section head, on what is required. You feel confident in your proven ability to manage each of these responsibilities effectively. However, you are not so happy about one other responsibility you have, namely, the monitoring of direct works expenditure on programmed projects, because not only are the direct labour section's estimates inaccurate but they are rarely stuck to anyway. This is a consistent source of friction between yourself and Dennis. From your previous experience as head of a small direct labour section you recognize the problem in viewing direct works in purely cost-effective terms, but you still feel sure that efficiency would be improved through tighter supervision, and the introduction of production bonus schemes for programmed project works. When you suggested this to Dennis he told you to let him manage his section his way as it was functioning perfectly well without your interference. In the face of Dennis's reluctance to listen you have asked your supervisory engineers to keep a close watch on the progress of direct works and whenever possible, to try to 'gee things up a bit'. You were not surprised to get the impression as the result of a conversation with Dennis yesterday that he is feeling a bit intimidated by the closer monitoring of his staff, but as far as you are concerned, some tightening up is required, either directly or indirectly. You are glad there is the opportunity today to explain your ideas to your boss, Edward Finch, and gain his support to put pressure on Dennis.

However, while you welcome the discussion with Edward you are a little apprehensive about any prolonged discussion with him in case the subject of expenditure authorization comes up. Your job brief requires that you seek Edward's authorization on any expenditure on programmed works and on emergency works over £500 – below that limit you may authorize expenditure but are expected to report it back to Edward. From day one you have had problems with delays in authorization of expenditure proposals. They seem to spend a long time in Edward's in-tray. As you operate on a tight budget with constantly changing priorities, and as you see it, you need to be able to take and act on decisions quickly if you are to be effective, Edward's 'leave it with me' style has been an increasing source of frustration and a real threat to your section's effectiveness.

In the last few months, however, you have found this frustration more 'liveable with' mainly as a result of some minor deviations from procedure which have occurred. Three months ago there was an occasion where you simply forgot to report back on the authorization of £450 for emergency safety work on a bridge parapet. When you remembered a week later it was obvious Edward was none the wiser and never would be as he rarely looked at detailed expenditure, so there seemed little point in bringing it up. Two weeks later you submitted a proposal as a result of a survey report for expenditure on fairly urgent sewer maintenance which involved the replacement of two sets of sewage pumping equipment. While the report was still awaiting Edward's authorization one pump failed so you brought in specialist contractors under emergency powers to replace the failed pump. You felt that since the contractors were there anyway, and in the interests of keeping costs down, you would ask them to replace the other set of pumps. You knew you were exceeding your authority at this point but intended to tell Edward as soon as possible. However, by the time Edward returned from a week's course it seemed like water under the bridge. He is in any case only really interested in 'the bottom line' as far as the budget is concerned so you decided to say no more about it, and to record the expenditure under emergency maintenance in the monthly financial report. Since then there have been several pieces of expenditure which, in the interests of keeping a fast turn around on the section you have authorized yourself and recorded under emergency maintenance. While you feel this has been in the best interests of not just your section, but the department as a whole, you do wonder whether you may have overstepped the mark with the authorization yesterday of £15,000 in excess of the planned programmed works on a road resurfacing contract. In fact on reflection you know you probably should report it, not least because it may make a large enough difference to the bottom line for Edward to pick it up.

You are about to have your staff development interview with Edward in accordance with the new staff development procedure just introduced into the department and are waiting outside his office.

Introduction

The cases of Peter Johnson and Maurice Bradley examine interpersonal skills in the appraisal interview situation. These two cases are intended to be used as *role play* situations which allow trainees to *practise* the analytical skills and communication skills necessary to conduct effective performance reviews.

Theory and background

The cases are vehicles for highlighting both analytical and communication skills of effective interpersonal behaviour. However, the primary focus in interpersonal skills (IPS) training is on *social process* and in our experience the use of role-played case studies requires that a trainer emphasizes the *communication* skills component and treats the analytical skills as secondary. Put another way, learning the skills necessary to *analyse* case *content* can jeopardize the learning of communication skills. This is particularly so if trainees seek to divert attention away from poor communication skills by initiating discussion (disagreements) about case content. Some attention must be given to analytical skills but we have found that generally these should be treated as subsidiary in the context of IPS training. The following notes reflect this view.

Analytical skills

It is widely accepted that a primary aim of appraisal is to develop the performance of a job holder (Randell *et al.* 1974). Individual performance is recognized to be a function of (a) *capacity* or *ability*, (b) *motivation* and (c) *environmental* (situational) *opportunities* and *constraints* (Cummings and Schwab, 1973). Therefore the objectives of a performance review interview can be constructed in terms of these three factors and the case material analysed in these terms.

Communication skills

Any skilled communicative performance involves *purposeful* sequences of *adaptive* and *timed* behaviours and is achieved through *practice* with *feedback*. In complex interpersonal situations such as the appraisal interview the skilled interviewer has to:

1 *Ask, listen, interpret* and *utilize* verbal and non-verbal information in a co-ordinated manner.
2 Be *flexible* in adapting style and direction to suit the situation, whilst maintaining an overall *sequence* and *structure* to the interview.
3 Be able to control the *pace* and *overall* length of the discussion.

Key learning points

The interviewee's brief for each case appear as appendices to these notes: Peter Johnson (Appendix 1); Maurice Bradley (Appendix 2).

Analytical skills

Trainees may be guided towards analysing substantive appraisal issues in the cases in terms of appraisee job performance being a function of ability, motivation and environmental opportunities and constraints. 'Corrected' analyses offered by the trainer are, in our experience, usually best avoided – the issues in the cases are intended as vehicles for addressing analytical skills and if the trainer's preferred analysis becomes a focus this can emphasize still further the problem of trainees' attention being diverted from communication processes, a problem which, as already mentioned, is often introduced in focusing on analytical skills at all.

Substantive appraisal issues in the two cases to which attention may particularly be drawn are:
Peter Johnson:
Peter Johnson's behaviour towards other members of the departmental management team.
His apparent competitiveness about the running of his own factory – he appears secretive and protective.
His informal approach to staff use of company resources.
What may be becoming an inappropriate relationship between Peter Johnson and marketing.
Maurice Bradley:
The possibility that Maurice Bradley may be exceeding his authority.

The possibility that he may be cutting corners or changing established routines.

What looks like being a relationship problem between Maurice Bradley and Denis Marshall, as well as between their respective sections.

Communication skills

In the nature of IPS training, learning is specific to individual trainees. Thus the identification of key learning points with respect to communication skills cannot be specified in advance, although pointers may be suggested. The following note offers some such suggestions. As has frequently been observed (Bailey and Butcher 1983 (a), (b); Wright and Taylor 1984 (a), (b)) identification of learning points and gaining the trainee's commitment to them is a demanding process requiring skilled behaviour from the trainer. Here we will confine ourselves to offering suggestions the trainer might use for *structuring* his/her *observation* of the appraisal interview in order to identify some key learning points.

Although individual trainers have preferred modes of analysis, in our experience of IPS training there is a wide range of conceptual tools that a trainer might use. The differences between these essentially reflect distinctions between levels of behavioural analysis. However, the appropriateness of any one level depends on the circumstance and so we will consider when these different levels of analysis are most appropriate.

Levels of analysis

Stages of the interview
Where achieving the interview objective relies on the achievement of subobjectives then it is always appropriate to monitor the degree of achievement of each subobjective. In appraisal interviews identifying a problem, an appropriate solution, and gaining commitment to action are distinguishable subobjectives.

Interview processes
Every interview involves an amount of information-gathering and information-giving but it is the interview purpose which dictates their correct balance. In appraisal interviews the emphasis is appropriately placed on information-sharing. Where interview purpose provides these basic guidelines then monitoring the balance of these processes is appropriate. Additionally, large individual differences exist in both the display and perception of non-verbal behaviour so where either becomes salient it is appropriate to monitor their effects.

Techniques and microskills

A more detailed analysis of interviewer behaviour focuses on questioning technique, listening skills and competence in dealing with feelings expressed by the interviewee. Different question types (e.g. open, closed, probes, etc.) are appropriate for seeking different types of information (Randell et al. 1974) and at different stages of the interview. Skilled interviewing therefore requires accurate and flexible use of question types and so it is appropriate to focus on questioning technique where rigidity is apparent or where questions fail to elicit the required information. Success also depends on the interviewer's ability to attend and appear to attend to the interviewee, and, in most interview situations, on his/her ability to both detect and respond appropriately to expressed feelings. It is always therefore important to reflect on whether the interviewer is listening and it is usually important to note whether expressed feelings are being dealt with. This level of analysis focuses on the basic components of effective communication and so it might be regarded as the most essential conceptual tool of the trainer.

Style of approach

Labels which describe the interviewer's style (e.g. authoritative, benevolent, consultative, democratic) are commonly used to encapsulate all the undertones and minute aspects of behaviour which indicate the interviewer's disposition to the interviewee. These tend to go hand-in-hand with the approaches (tell and tell, tell and sell, ask and listen, etc.) which are described as appraisal interview types (Maier 1958). While such modes of behaviour are often indicative of preferred personal style, skilled interviewing calls for style and approach flexibility. In particular, the purpose and stage of the interview, as well as the interviewee's behaviour and expectations, determine which style or approach will be most effective. In cases where rigidity of style or approach have a poor effect or where the adopted style contradicts these situational requirements then this macro-level of analysis provides a useful starting point for analysing performance.

It is apparent that the utility of each of these four conceptual tools is in some sense situationally dependent. But while they can be distinguished from one another we refer to them as levels of analysis because they are not mutually exclusive. Rather, they are different ways of structuring observation such that significant behaviours might be picked up at several of these analytical levels. For example, an authoritarian style is often manifest through the use of leading questions, a tell-tell approach, lack of listening, a predominance of information-giving etc. (Wright and Taylor 1981). Because of this overlap the trainer is able to analyse performance in a variety of ways. This is important because it allows flexibility in giving feedback where, by taking account of trainee ability, knowledge and receptiveness, the feedback can be expressed in terms which are likely to be both understood and accepted. This potential benefit signals a need for the trainer to be adept at working at these different levels. In addition, this facility is required because, on occasion, significant behaviours are not perceptible at all levels – to take a simple example, an authoritarian style is not always accompanied by a predominance of information-giving. Clearly then, flexibility in the use of these conceptual tools is advantageous and this summary is intended to provide the trainer with an aide-memoire of the main types.

Teaching guide summary

Issues

1. Analytical skills:
Substantive appraisal issues in the two case studies
(a) Peter Johnson
(b) Maurice Bradley.

2. Communication skills?
Learning points specific to individual trainees drawn from their interpersonal performance in the role plays.

Learning points

- Distinguishing between causes of appraisee performance in terms of
ability
motivation
environmental
opportunities
constraints.

- Behavioural learning identified using the suggested 'levels of analysis' framework
stages of the interview (achievment of subobjectives)
interview processes (information giving/gathering, display/perception of non-verbal behaviour)
micro-skills (questioning technique, listening, dealing with expressed feelings)
style/approach.

Teaching style

Taylor (1986), in discussing the role of an appraisal interviewing tutor, made distinction between directive and causal-analytic tutoring styles suggesting that the latter is the more appropriate in giving feedback. While in basic agreement, we have found that both approaches have their value and so here we will review the relative merits of these tutoring styles.

The causal-analytic style

When the trainer explores interview events with observers and the interviewer by seeking a description of interviewer behaviour and interviewee reactions, eliciting suggestions for alternative behaviours and exploring the likely effectiveness of these he/she is adopting a causal-analytic style. The style is essentially participative and we have summarized its relative merits in Table 1. In general, providing the trainer is skilled at questioning and group control, the advantages appear to outweigh the disadvantages.

The directive style

When the trainer describes the performance event, telling the trainee what he/she did wrong, why behaviour was ineffective, and how to behave more effectively, a directive style is being adopted. In stating his/her covert performance analysis the trainer is seeking to alter behaviour by persuasion or at least by authority based on expertise. The underlying assumptions of this style do not always hold and this is reflected in its disadvantages. Although it would appear that disadvantages outweigh advantages there are circumstances (e.g. lack of time or where trainees lack analytical ability) when the directive style is appropriate and effective *if* the trainer is skilled in analysis and persuasion.

As with interviewing itself, there is no one best way nor one correct style of giving feedback. Style appropriateness depends on the situation, the particular trainee and the trainer's skills. Flexibility of style, then, is the key to effectiveness here. While one or other will be preferred, trainers need to recognize the limitations of each style and the implied demands on their skills.

In our own view, although the directive style clearly can be useful, in terms of achieving the objective of facilitating the development of communication skills the causal-analytic style is generally both more effective and more elegant. The extra time invested can be expected to show a return in the trainee's commitment to behavioural change and an ability to continue skill development.

Table 1 *The relative merits of tutoring styles*

Causal-analytic	Directive
Advantages	
Nurtures self analysis.	Uses time economically.
Nurtures self feedback.	Preferred by authority seeking trainees.
Enhances commitment to change.	Suited to low analytical ability trainees.
Provides practice for observer analysis.	
Utilizes observer resources.	
Disadvantages	
Relatively time-consuming.	More likely to achieve compliance *vs* commitment.
Inappropriate for low analytical ability trainees.	Increased likelihood of resistance.
Frustrates 'plain-speaking' trainees	Inappropriate for high analytical ability trainees.
Requires high level questioning and group control skills of the trainer.	Wasteful of observer resources.
	Requires high level analytical and persuasion skills of the trainer.

References

C. T. Bailey and D. J. Butcher, 'Interpersonal Skills Training I: The Nature of Skill Acquisition and its Implications for Training Design and Management', *Management Education and Development*, Vol. 14, No. 1, 1983a, pp. 48–54.

C. T. Bailey and D. J. Butcher, 'Interpersonal Skills Training II: The Trainer's Role', *Management Education and Development*, Vol. 14, No. 2, 1983b, pp. 106–12.

L. L. Cummings and D. P. Schwab, *Performance in Organizations – Determinants and Appraisal*, Scott Foresman, 1973.

N. F. R. Maier, 'Three Types of Appraisal Interview', *Personnel*, Vol. 34, No. 5, 1958, pp. 27–40.

G. A. Randell, P. M. A. Packard, R. L. Shaw and A. J. Slater, '*Staff Appraisal*' (Revised Edition), Institute of Personnel Management, 1974.

D. S. Taylor, '*Performance Reviews: A Handbook for Tutors*', Institute of Personnel Management, 1976.

P. L. Wright and D. S. Taylor, 'The Interpersonal Skills of Leadership; Their Analysis and Training II', *Leadership and Organization Development Journal*, Vol. 2, No. 3, 1981, pp. 2–6.

P. L. Wright and D. S. Taylor, 'The Development of Tutoring Skills for Interpersonal Skills Trainers', *Journal of European Industrial Training*, Vol. 8, No. 6, 1984a, pp. 27–33.

P. L. Wright and D. S. Taylor, 'Hiccups and Nightmares: Some Problems in Tutoring Role Play Exercises', *Journal of European Industrial Training*, Vol. 8, No. 7, 1984b, pp. 25–31.

SEVEN

The Industrial Development Authority

ANDREW P. KAKABADSE

Introduction

The case of the Industrial Development Authority examines *interpersonal behaviour* at senior management levels in an organization. It can be used to highlight key aspects of managerial behaviour and to indicate the *practical* difficulties of *introducing* management development to any organization.

Theory and background

The case examines *hostility* and *conflict* between executives of a public sector organization. It highlights the importance of *politics in organizations*. Organizational politics is interpreted as the *ability to act* and interact effectively in various situations. Certain writers such as Mangham (1979) imply that behaviour considered as political should be considered a *necessary evil* and hence such behaviour should be applied only when all other approaches are considered *ineffective*. Kakabadse and Parker (1984(b)) *refute* the assertion that politics involves behaviours considered as undesirable but necessary. They consider that people are capable of *learning* to respond, react and utilize their surrounding environment and hence are *capable of choice* and *self-regulation*. In this way, human beings develop their particular *frames of reference* which drives their behaviour through their subjective interpretation of social interaction (Bandura 1977; Mischel 1977; Goffman 1974). Based on this notion, Kakabadse and Parker (1984(a)) view politics as an *influence process* which can be perceived as *positive* (motivating) or *negative* (undesirable) depending on whether one's frame(s) of reference is supported or threatened. In this way, all behaviour in organizations *holds political connotations*. Hence, in order to address sensitive issues, it is important to appreciate the views and values of individuals and the shared norms, or *culture(s)* of organization (Kakabadse 1982; Brakel 1985; Schein 1985), which may determine certain predominantly held attitudes. Such understanding is invaluable in assisting individuals to *negotiate outcomes* that are to their satisfaction or at least can be tolerated. The ways of *handling conflict*, organizational *politics* and *disagreement* are outlined in the case analysis.

Key learning points

The case concentrates on the fortunes of one senior executive, Henry Mitchell, and his attempts to introduce change and improve managerial performance in the Industrial Development Authority (IDA). In particular the following points, during case discussion, need to be drawn to the students' attention:

1 Positional opportunities and constraints.
2 Stakeholder analysis.
3 Culture of organization.
4 The role of the change agent.

Positional opportunities and constraints

The managerial position/role held by individuals provides *opportunities* to pursue particular objectives that may or may not be part of the executive's direct role/organizational responsibilities. The case indicates that the skills of *negotiation* and the *ability to influence* others are key considerations for *effective managerial performance*. Draw to the class's attention the behaviour of the following individuals:

● Henry Mitchell's attempt to *influence* Jim Carthy after the submission of the second report indicating that if the IDA was to be effective, redundancies would be necessary. Carthy's objections to the report were overcome by Mitchell through him influencing his boss by emphasizing the potential personal recognition for Carthy if the re-organization was successful.

● The *strategies* adopted by Green and Davidson in terms of secretly keeping the personality test scores of managers attending inter-personal skills programmes and putting together a hitlist of undesired managers for Mitchell to transfer out of their job or organization.

● Ray Leonard's successful attempts to influence Carthy to appoint him as Director of Personnel.

However, holding a senior management role also involves effectively managing *problems* and *constraints*. The constraints involve simultaneously managing situations in which executives hold *conflicting needs and objectives* for which no easy solution exists, *gaining* and *maintaining* credibility amongst senior colleagues and bosses and simply recognizing that any senior executive is *vulnerable*. Use the following examples to highlight these points.

- Carthy's *sponsorship* of Henry Mitchell to Director of Business Development in the knowledge of Didson's disapproval of Mitchell. Further, Carthy's support of Didson as Head of Manpower Services, recognizing the problems that Mitchell would have to face, are examples of conflicting situations for which no easy solutions exist. In all probability, Carthy believed that both men were the right appointments for their respective positions. His public support for Mitchell on appointment to Director of Business Development was, more than likely, sincerely made. With such tensions in the situation, Carthy discovered he could not apply his influence as he desired.

- Mitchell's *judgement* in accepting the post of Director of Business Development needs to be questioned. Although recognizing the difficulties he would likely have with the civil servants in the Department of Industry, he does not seem to have fully thought through the implication of working closer to Didson. Further, he seems to have made little attempt to try to work closer with Didson when Didson was appointed Head of Manpower Services. Perhaps Mitchell considered it impossible to negotiate a closer working relationship with Didson. Mitchell's judgement again needs to be questioned when he realized that he did not, or would not, have Carthy's support concerning pressure from Didson. Mitchell portrays a picture of a person who is naive concerning senior managerial relationships. He does not readily seem to have appreciated the *vulnerability* faced by senior managers.

Stakeholder analysis

The *views, values and objectives* of individuals in any managerial situation require analysis. Individuals who can substantially influence the situation such as Didson, Carthy, Mitchell and Leonard are termed *stakeholders*. These individuals have a stakeholding or *strong interest* in the situation. The interests and intentions of stakeholders, require *examination* so as to identify the *pressures* and *tensions shaping* the situation. Explore the positions adopted and the personal values of key managers such as Carthy, who reluctantly felt it necessary to instigate change into the IDA whilst attempting to maintain some cohesion in his management team by appeasing Leonard and in trying to support the right man for the right job – Mitchell – in both posts of Director of Personnel and Business Development. Further, Carthy recognized and backed Didson as a person of considerable skill and talent while recognizing the inevitable problems in the Didson/Mitchell relationship. The assumption behind a stakeholder analysis is that the formation of policies and strategies in an organisation is as much subjective as objective; it is much dependent on rational thinking and data as on influential individuals' personal beliefs, values and ideals as to what the organization should be doing externally, and its manner of organization internally. Stakeholder analysis highlights the political processes of decision making and policy generation in an organization.

Negotiating deals and coming to an 'understanding' are considered important factors in terms of managing conflicting stakeholder demands. As stated, executives can find themselves in situations where they are managing conflicting interests. The advantages of pursuing a particular course of action need to be carefully considered especially if the person needs to choose between alternatives. Mitchell's discussion with his wife (at end of case) indicates that Carthy ceased his support for Mitchell in order not to be perceived in a negative light by Didson. In effect, Carthy traded his relationship with Mitchell for that of Didson's.

The *emotional cost* of managing working relationships in this way, can be high. If the relationship between two executives has largely been founded on *trust*, it may be difficult for one or both parties to come to terms with the change of relationship. Reference is made to this at the end of the case in the conversation between Mitchell and his wife. Evelyn Mitchell found the subtle change of relationship difficult to comprehend, whereas Mitchell indicates greater under-standing of the situation by his analysis of Carthy's position. Explore with the class what Carthy may feel by not backing one of his ablest directors.

Belief in rationality. A common assumption held by managers is 'an individual will be *aptly rewarded* for work *well done.*' The case challenges the validity of the assumption and provides examples of individuals influencing others in order to achieve particular out-comes, such as Green and Davidson's attempts to influence Mitchell, Leonard's discussions with Carthy in order to achieve a change of role, and Mitchell's influencing of Carthy to accept and implement the second report. Despite *recognizing* that the *ability to influence* is an important element of achieving a successful outcome, Mitchell still displays some surprise at feeling let down by Carthy. Explore with the class whether this is naïvety on Mitchell's part or a more fundamental element of people's belief system that reward and successful endeavour are held synonymous. Highlight that success is not simply dependent on task accomplishment. *Numerous criteria* exist for successful executive performance.

Culture of organization

Culture of organization refers to the *norms*, *attitudes* and *behaviour* that become the distinguishing characteristics of an organization, such as the management and supervisory styles, flow of communications, sharing of information and attitudes towards conformity and non-conformity. The concept of culture encompasses the *perceptions* and *feelings people share* about each other and their work situation. It should not be assumed that one prevailing culture dominates an organization for different ideals and points of view are likely to exist between those working in research and development, marketing, Production and Personnel Departments.

The class should be encouraged to state their views as to the shared norms of behaviour and attitudes among management in the IDA and if possible arrive with a word or phrase which epitomizes the culture(s) of the organization. Key elements of culture to highlight are:

• The *individualistic* nature to *decision making*, largely dependent on each person's *skills of influence*. Note the manner in which Green and Davidson influence Mitchell with their hitlist; also examine Mitchell's assessment of Carthy in order to have the general report accepted; also Leonard's successful influence attempts to obtain Carthy's support to change functions in the organization.

• Managers *not used* to being held *accountable* for their performance. This can be deduced from the comments made on the first report and the reasons for Green and Davidson's emphasis on project work, action planning and team building.

• *Lack of trust* between managers, partly dependent on the individualistic approach to influencing others and decision making, and on the inability to practise accountability as a performance assessment measure. Examples of lack of trust are given in the first report, the relationship between Leonard and Tony Rivers, and Carthy taking risks with Mitchell's future in encouraging him to accept a job which would expose him to Didson.

• *Unclear criteria for executive performance*. In fact the ability to influence others to gain one's own objectives is the strong emerging criteria. Note Mitchell's influence on Carthy, Leonard's influence on Carthy, Carthy's support for Didson and the possible influence Didson may have had on Carthy. Although it is not stated in the case, the ability to influence others needs to be emphasized as an important practised criteria for performance.

● *Difference of values between middle and senior management* as highlighted in the first report and in the different reactions to the training programmes. Understandably, middle management found it difficult to trust and identify with senior management if the organization lacked clear corporate objectives and did not practise fundamental managerial principles such as being held accountable for performance or appointment to positions based on skills and abilities.

● *External organizational pressures* influenced the thinking and attitudes of senior management. The IDA was exposed to civil servant influence and hence internal direction concerning future direction and appointment of key personnel had to be taken with the civil servants in mind. Highlight the personalized nature of external influence. The civil servants did not directly involve themselves in policy formation but acted in the minds of the IDA executives as a veto and also attempted to influence the appointment or departure of particular individuals to key posts.

● The IDA displays an *inward* looking culture and does not seem to structure itself or be sensitive to external community/market demands. This was highlighted in the report and is also the reason for the project and team building emphasis to the training programmes.

The role of change the agent
Mitchell acts as the change agent for the IDA. He *master-minded* the change programme, *substantially influenced* Carthy and attempted to set about *improving* the Business Development Directorate. Mitchell occupied the role of *internal change agent*. Emphasize the following characteristics of the internal change agent.

● The internal consultant/change agent is far more *accessible* to other managers in the organization than an externally hired consultant. This makes him more easily accountable for the intervention. Hence, risk on the change agent's part may be reduced if he attempts to ensure that the intervention is perceived as successful, or at least not a failure.

● The internal change agent is likely to have *greater potential access* to people and information and thereby likely to hold greater insight and understanding of the culture(s) of the organization.

● The internal change agent may *lack the mystique* and *credibility* that may be attributed to external agents. Other managers in the organization may not give sufficient attention to their internal agent or the issues could be too threatening for the internal agent to address, or the internal consultant may not be considered sufficiently expert. Hence, external consultants could be hired to provide a similar service.

The important point to emphasize is that the internal agent is *more at risk* for he cannot call a halt to the intervention without possibly losing face or his job in the organization.

Teaching guide summary

Issues	Learning points
1 Organizational position.	● Personal opportunities. ● Need to influence. ● Identify strategies of influence. ● Constraints. ● Manage contradictory demands simultaneously. ● Credibility maintenance. ● Executive vulnerability. ● Executive judgement.
2 Stakeholder analysis.	● Individual values and objectives. ● Subjective/objective nature to policy formation. ● Negotiating deals. ● Emotional cost of negotiating deals. ● Belief in rationality. ● Relationship between reward and performance.

3 Culture of organization.	● Shared norms and attitudes.
	● Numerous cultures in one organization.
	● Elements of culture in IDA are:
	    individualistic
	    lack of accountability
	    lack of trust

		unclear criteria for executive performance
		values clash between middle and senior management
		external organizational influences
		inward looking culture.
4 Role of change agent.	•	Internal agent gives different dynamics to external consultant in terms of:
		access to managers
		more easily accountable
		less risk taking
		greater internal access
		greater insight and understanding
		possible lack of mystique and credibility.

This summary can be formally prepared for acetate or flip-chart presentation, and used for providing a comprehensive summary at the end of case discussion.

Teaching style

Make available three white boards/black boards, or three flip charts, or 1 flip-chart pad with the facility to Blutack three or four flip-chart sheets to a wall.

Ask the groups to present the results of their discussion of each question. Write on the flip chart the key findings of each group. After the groups have finished their presentations, fit their findings into the structure of the teaching guide on a separate board. As the key points of organizational position, stakeholder analysis, culture of organization and role of change agent are being presented on flip chart/white board encourage discussion with the class, exploring whether they recognize these key points in the case.

In the closing summary of the case, highlight the importance of interpersonal skills as a means to negotiating increased personal influence, an essential feature of the political nature of life in organizations.

References

A. Bandura, *Social Learning Theory*. (Prentice Hall, 1977).
A. Brakel, (ed.) *People and Organisations Interacting* (John Wiley, 1985).

E. Goffman, *Frame Analysis: An Essay on The Organisation of Experience*, (Penguin, 1974).

A. P. Kakabadse, *Culture of the Social Services*, (Gower, 1982).

A. P. Kakabadse and C. Parker, 'Towards a Theory of Political Behaviour in Organisation,' in Kakabadse and Parker (Eds) *Power, Politics and Organisation: A Behavioural Science View*, (John Wiley, 1984(a)).

A. P. Kakabadse and C. Parker, 'The Undiscovered Dimensions of Management Education: Politics in Organisations,' in Cox and Beck *Management Development: Advances in Practice and Theory*, (John Wiley, 1984(b)).

I. Mangham, *The Politics of Organisational Change*, (Associated Business Press, 1979).

W. Mischel, 'Self-control of the Self', in Mischel T. (Ed) *The Self: Psychological and Philosophical Issues*, (Rundinan & Littlefield, 1977).

E. H. Schein, *Organisational Culture and Leadership*, (Jossey Bass, 1985).

EIGHT

Guy Roberts

RON LUDLOW

Introduction

The case of Guy Roberts examines the socialization process and the power and influence of groups specifically looking at norms of behaviour and the effect of peer pressure on individual values and needs.

Theory and background

The analysis of this case will provide an opportunity to explore individual value differences within groups, to see the ways in which they are resolved in groups and with what consequences. Ideally, groups should be formed in good time for norms to be established, then individuals and the group can identify with problems which are similar to those faced by Guy Roberts in this case.

Organizational socialization is the process of transforming newly selected members into a state of full participation and effectiveness within the organization. This may involve changes of attitudes and values of the new members while they are adjusting to their new jobs, work groups, organizational systems and structures. It is a period of learning and mutual adaptation between the new member and his manager in particular.

In the case of Guy Roberts at Millard's, it is clear that the early organizational learning period is extremely critical in the formation of new values, new attitudes and new behaviours. Within his group there is a strong norm to continue an illegal practice which is followed without question by other members of the group. If Guy does not conform to this norm he will be labelled a deviant and be subject to peer pressure from within the group to conform. He has the choice of remaining true to his own values or observing the norm. His choice therefore has consequences for both himself and for the organization.

Key learning points

1 Individual values and needs.
2 The socialization process and transition – group influences.
3 Group norms.
4 Group conformity.

Individual values and needs

The conflict of values and needs is key to appreciating this section. The case portrays Guy Roberts as a well-qualified and competent quantity surveyor, married, with a small baby. His financial commitments include a high mortgage. He is the sole breadwinner, and therefore redundancy can be seen as not only a potential shock to his morale, but also a very real financial worry. He desperately needs the Millard Construction job.

When his values are challenged at Millard's, he is forced to subjugate his moral principles to the more practical fulfilment of his financial needs. However, Guy has two moral challenges: the first involving the fraudulent disposal of Millard's building materials by the foreman and his senior quantity surveyer, and the second relating to the presentation of false petrol claims. He is also presented with a challenge to his estimating ability, which poses a threat to his technical competence.

Things are further complicated by the fact that Guy's senior quantity surveyor is also his brother-in-law. Therefore, at work and at home he is under pressure to conform.

When Guy's estimating ability is challenged, he defends his bill of quantities. However, on finding out that it is the 'norm' at Millard's to add on a percentage to cover accidental loss or damage, he backs down, realizing that 'he is not in any position to argue.' (Note the change in his attitude, however, when he finds out what is happening to some of the excess materials. He reverts to his original position, defends his estimates and insists on their implementation.)

He steadfastly refuses to have anything to do with the fraudulent conversion of Millard's building materials. Initially, he also refuses to take part in the 'petrol fiddle,' because it is offered to him at the time he discovers the materials fraud.

He does agree to keep quiet about the dishonest practices, partly because his name is on the 'adjusted' bill of quantities, which, as Neville insinuates, could look like collusion in the event of an enquiry.

Group influence in the socialization process

Guy's refusal to take part in the two fraudulent practices at Millard's puts him in a position of social isolation. His fellow quantity surveyors will not speak to him unless they have to. He is therefore an outcast among his peers. He begins to lose pleasure in his job.

His senior quantity surveyor and the yard foreman treat him in a similar manner. However the mental stress this causes is soon compounded by incidents which cause Guy to suffer actual physical loss.

His petrol claims are 'lost' (clearly Neville is responsible for this), which causes Guy financial stress. His car is 'damaged' by the foreman, driving the dumper truck. This forces Guy to spend more time getting to work on public transport, and curtails his company visits. His time is not being used efficiently, therefore he cannot function effectively.

Guy is under pressure to conform – the group is exerting mental and physical pressure.

Then, his estimating ability is once more challenged – this time by the manager. Materials have actually run out. Later on, materials fail to arrive on time. Guy has now been given two valid reason for 'over-ordering.'

Finally, we find that he is under pressure at home. His wife pleads with him to say nothing about Neville's dishonesty 'for the sake of family unity.' She also believes that he is in danger of losing his job, as he is still working through his three-month trial period and 'Millards are far from happy with Guy's performance.' She advises him to see Neville in order to come to a better working arrangement.

Guy realizes that he must conform. He has lost peer-group approval, the support of his senior quantity surveyor (his brother-in-law, Neville), the cooperation of the yard foreman, and the respect of senior management. He has no pleasure or satisfaction in his job, and stands in danger of being dismissed. However, he simply cannot afford to lose his job, because of his financial position.

Norms of behaviour and the effect of peer pressure

At Millard Construction, Guy has found that fraud is an accepted norm. Initially, however, his values make it impossible for him to conform. Peer group pressure inside and outside work, however, brings him to the point where he has to compromise or get out. He therefore agrees to add 10 per cent to his bills of quantities. After all, he has been shown a very valid reason for doing so, by the Company Manager. His personal financial difficulties combine with peer group pressure to make him agree to take part in the petrol claim 'fiddle.'

However, he will not take part in the fraudulent disposal of materials. Yet, for the sake of a more harmonious working atmosphere between himself, Neville, and the yard foreman, he does agree to say nothing to senior management about the fraud. It could therefore be argued that, by keeping silent, he condones the fraud.

However, the incongruence between Guy's values and the group norms is likely to have an adverse effect on him. It is difficult to see him being an effective employee at Millard's in the medium- and long-term. The knowledge that he is playing both an active and a passive role in cheating the company out of money will, in time, demotivate him because it is in conflict with his normal standards of behaviour.

This is the sort of situation that many managers face in transition and in the socialization process, where their personal values conflict with those of the organizational culture into which they move; where they have to compromise their values because of their need for companionship and approval, which they cannot afford to lose.

Teaching guide summary

Issues	Learning points
1 Socialization.	• The need for a fit between the individual, the job, and the organization.
	• Problems of entry and socialization.
	• Adjusting to new jobs, new co-workers, new organizational structures, systems, and practices.
	• Changing values and attitudes.
	• Developing new work skills.
	• Developing new behaviours.
	• Learning organizational values.
	• Importance of initial experiences.
	• Developing new interpersonal relationships.
	• Developing new work norms.

2 Values and needs.
- Individual value systems.
- Relative importance of individual values.
- Group values and norms.
- Individual needs:
  basic existence and survival
  social and acceptance
  growth and development.
- At what levels of needs are individuals working?
- Potential conflicts between values and needs:
  external factors
  internal dissonance

3 Group norms.
- Guidelines for appropriate behaviour in groups.
- Task-related, maintenance-related, group-related, individual-related.
- Restrictions in output.
- Costs of deviant behaviour.
- Pressure to conform.
- Group cohesiveness.
  social isolation
  non-cooperative behaviour
  antagonistic behaviour.

Teaching style

Make available white boards/black boards, or flip charts. Ask the groups to present the results of their discussion of each question on flip charts if possible. After the groups have finished their presentations, summarize the key findings of each group and relate to the structure of the teaching guide on a separate board. Encourage discussion with the class exploring whether they recognise and identify these key points from the case.

In the closing summary of the case, emphasize the importance of effective socialization processes in organizations to improve managerial effectiveness, the conflicts that will inevitably arise between individual and organizational values, and the power of the work group in enforcing individual conformity to group norms.

NINE

Grayle Engineering

RON LUDLOW

Introduction

The case of Grayle Engineering examines the roles and activities of a middle manager in an organization. It can be used to highlight the practical difficulties a manager encounters in attempting to plan, coordinate, organize, and control his work in any organization.

Theory and background

The case examines the reactive nature of a manager's work in a manufacturing organization. It highlights the difficulties that managers face in organizing their time to carry out long-term planning. Mintzberg (1973) suggested that the classical view of the manager's job proposed by Henri Fayol in 1916, whereby a manager plans, organizes, coordinates, and controls is not borne out by the facts which emerged from his study of what managers actually did in their work context. His work indicates that although managers retained these four major functions as vague objectives which they have when at work, an analysis of the activities and roles of the manager as observed, and a synthesis of available research, indicated that a manager fulfils ten fragmentary roles when at work. The case also highlights another way of analysing managerial work, that of Stewart (1976), by looking at the choices, demands, and constraints which influence the work which a manager does, and the way in which he structures his work.

Key learning points

The case concentrates on the work of one manager, Norman Graham, during one day at Grayle Engineering. In particular the following points, during class discussion should be drawn to the students' attention:

1 Analysis of managerial work.
2 Influences on managerial behaviour.
3 Change strategies for improving managerial effectiveness.

Analysis of managerial work

Norman Graham is a middle manager in Grayle Engineering. His background is in engineering and he has had very little formal training in management. We follow him through a typical day in his working life. As with most managers there is a large variance in what he intends to do that day, and what he actually does. He intends to initiate major action to ensure that his ideas to expand the Electrical Department by 'going commercial' can really get off the ground, but is forced into a 'fire fighting' role because of the short-term pressures he faces during the day.

Norman has formal authority within the company and has the intention of using this to work through the management process of planning, organizing, leading, and controlling, but the limits of his authority are such that he cannot make effective planning or operational decisions without working with a network of contacts throughout the company on whom he relies for information, and by the use of informal influence and the norm of reciprocity can make things happen.

The manner in which he behaves as a manager is mostly reactive, that is, he solves short-term problems (many of which are not even his problems). It could be described as 'hands-on' management rather than strategic management. Management by exception is not for him: he gets involved in what is going on, whether it is his concern or not. His day is filled with interruptions for decisions on problems the solution for which he has not delegated, nor in many cases belong to his department anyway. He appears to have a need for constant verbal communication but uses no effective management information system within the formal organization, although his own personal network of contacts provides him with the information he needs to carry out his job. His has an 'open-door' style; a method of management by walking around.

An appropriate method for analysing and describing his managerial style is that annotated by Mintzberg. Norman Graham, throughout the day, performs in all the ten roles described by Mintzberg. The emphasis of assessment of his performance appears to be on his decision making roles; however, to be effective in these roles he needs adequate and relevant information, and to obtain this information he needs to be effective in his interpersonal roles, for which purpose he uses his network of informal contacts within the organization.

Influences on managerial behaviour

There are many reasons why Norman Graham behaves as he does in his managerial role. Although he wants to think long term and plan more with respect to 'going commerical', he is forced into short-term decision making and problem solving by such factors as the constraining structure of the organization and his own ill-defined areas of authority and accountability.

His previous experience was primarily that of an electrical engineer – he appears to be acting more as a supervisor still rather than as a manager. He is undoubtedly going through a transition into his new position, and with very little managerial training to date, he is not aware that the major role of a manager is to get work done through other people, not do that work himself.

The pressures within the organization and particularly on Norman Graham are on today's crises, not planning for tomorrow.

Norman is very much a people person, with intense interest in his subordinates' and his colleagues' problems. Because of his concern for people and his interest in them, he is willing, and in some cases, actively searches out, reasons for being interrupted in his primary work.

The role of Norman's boss is of interest. Norman appears to spend very little time with his boss, who appears to be letting Norman get on with solving short-term problems, and not giving any direction or control in order to help Norman delegate some of these problems, and so allow him more discretionary time to carry out his long-term planning.

Norman's personality requires analysis and discussion. The choices Norman makes in relation to the way in which he carries out his job, within the demands and constraints already imposed upon him, are very much affected by his high people-orientation. He likes to work and to deal with people; he likes to solve other peoples' problems as well as his own; and he actively chooses to do this to the detriment of issues such as 'going commercial' which, although they are of importance to him both with respect to the organization and he himself as a manager, take a low priority with respect to the satisfaction he gains from interacting with other people. He enjoys being a 'fixer' rather than a planner.

Change strategies for improving Norman's managerial effectiveness

Norman's major problem is that of effective time/priority management. He tends to structure his time to do the things he wants to do, not the things he ought to do. He needs some assistance from his boss, or some training, in time management.

He needs an incentive to achieve his long-term priorities, to get his long-term jobs done. However, this means that he requires more discretionary time in order to carry out these tasks. Some ways in which this can be done are as follows:

• Regular consultation meetings instead of the 'open-door' policy which he adopts which mean that he is continuously being interrupted in his work.

• Recruiting more senior engineers into this section to share his workload: however, is this likely to be cost-effective?

• *Real* delegation to his subordinate engineers. However, this means that he has to decide how much real delegation he can give to his subordinates; perhaps some form of training, and/or risk taking by Norman Graham is necessary to help develop his subordinates so that part of his workload can be taken from him by them, so giving him more discretionary time to carry out his long-term tasks. Norman's perception of his role in his present managerial post appears to be very fuzzy. A greater clarity of his job description, accountability, and limits of authority, backed up by closer support from his boss, might solve this problem.

• Above all, Norman needs to plan both his time and his work realistically.

The changes which can be made fall into three categories:

1 Changes in structure/design.
2 Changes in systems.
3 Changes in people/styles of behaviour.

Inevitably, changes in one of these categories will have consequent effects on the others. Changes in structure may affect the systems which already exist in Grayle Engineering, which may affect either the type of people required to work within the systems and structure, or the styles of behaviour of people who already exist within the system.

Teaching guide summary

Issues	*Learning points*

1 Managerial work.	• The management process:
	    planning
	    organizing
	    leading
	    controlling.

	• Managerial roles:
	    interpersonal roles
	    information roles
	    decisional roles

	• Organizational and managerial demands and constraints.
	• Managerial choices at work.
2 Managerial styles.	• Reactive/proactive.
	• Management by exception
	• Management by walking around.
	• Open-door/democratic management
	• Concern for people/concern for task/things.
	• Hands-on management.
3 Influences on managerial behaviour.	• Constraining structures.
	• Limited and unclear areas of authority/ accountability/ responsibility.
	• Previous experiences and background.
	• Transitions into new managerial roles.
	• Personality.
	• Pressures for short-term results.
	• Planning for tomorrow.
	• The role of the manager's boss.
	• Management training and development.
	• Job and personal satisfaction.
	• Operational systems in organizations.

- The people with whom the manager works.
- Unclear job definition.
- Unclear criteria for performance.
- Incentives for long-term planning and delegation.

4 Strategies for improving time/priority managerial effectiveness.

- Management.
- Real delegation to subordinates.
- Training and development of subordinates.
- Recruitment of assistance/ colleagues to share workloads.
- Realistic planning.
- Support and guidance by the manager's boss.
- Induction and training into new managerial positions.
- Incentives to structure and increase discretionary time for long-term activities.

5 Categorization of change strategies.

- Structure/design.
- Systems.
- People/styles of behaviour.

6 Managerial dilemmas.

- Structuring and prioritizing time and effort to balance short term (e.g. problem solving, trouble shooting) and long-term (e.g. budgeting, planning, forecasting) activities at work.
- Company environment and own personality tend generally to move managers from long-term work to short-term work from which they get immediate feedback.
- Implications for job design.

This summary can be formally prepared for acetate flip-chart presentation, and used for providing a comprehensive summary at the end of class discussion.

Teaching style

Make available three white boards/black boards, or three flip charts.

1 First, ask the class to evaluate Norman Graham as a manager (they are members of an appraising board). Would they give him a pay rise of:

Above average	Average	Below average
worth 10%	5%	3%

List and keep a record of their evaluation.

2 Explore reasons for their assessment and list these reasons below the assessments themselves.

3 Ask the groups to describe Norman Graham's managerial style/behaviour – e.g. reactive, management by walking around, open-door, democratic, hands-on, etc.

4 Ask the groups to explain why Norman Graham behaves as he does and list these factors on the white board/black board/ flip charts.

5 Ask the groups to describe what Norman Graham does positively, and what he isn't so good at.

6 Relate all that has gone before to the management process, managerial roles, and organizational and managerial demands, choices, and constraints.

7 Ask the groups what changes can be made to help Norman improve his effectiveness as a manager. List these changes and change strategies.

8 Relate these changes which can be made to the three major categories of changes in structure/design, changes in systems, and changes in people/styles of behaviour.

9 Ask the class to consider the classic managerial dilemma which faces Norman Graham i.e. short-term versus long-term priorities and activities. Explore whether they recognize this key dilemma in their own jobs.

10 In the closing summary of the case, ask the class to consider their own jobs, and particularly the change strategies which they can implement to improve their own managerial effectiveness. At this stage go back to the class's original assessment of Norman Graham as a manager and consider the class's changes in perception.

References

H. Mintzberg, *The Nature of Managerial Work*, (Harper and Row, 1973).

R. Stewart, *Contrasts in Management: A Study of Different Types of Managers' Jobs, Their Demands and Choices*, (McGraw Hill, 1976).

TEN

The Youth Training Scheme

RON LUDLOW

Introduction

The case of The Youth Training Scheme examines interpersonal communication and the problems which occur when the sender's intended meaning is dissimilar to the receiver's perceived meaning. It can be used to highlight key aspects of both interpersonal and interfunctional communication problems within any organization.

Theory and background

The case examines miscommunications which occur when the sender and the receiver do not have a common understanding of the message. Miscommunications can occur when the sender chooses the wrong channel for his communication, when there is 'noise' in the system or when there is no adequate feedback channel between the receiver and the sender, when there are cultural differences between the receiver and the sender, and when the sender may deliberately send an unclear message, etc.

Today's complex organizations, operating in unstable environments, need an unprecedentedly high level of effective communication than has occurred in the past. This case illustrates examples of three common different types of miscommunication and of failure to communicate within any organization and the consequences of these miscommunications for organizational and personal performance:

1　Apparent agreement.
2　Deliberate miscommunication.
3　Cultural differences in word meanings.

Apparent agreement

The first illustration shows apparent agreement over a written communication. Marion Lane tells her young secretary to send out letters to all trainees in the YTS Retail Training Group informing them of the day trip to London. The miscommunication occurs over the different meanings which the sender and the receivers attach to the word *station*. Marion's young secretary has omitted to qualify the noun, 'station', by the adjective, 'railway'. To her, the meaning is obvious, partly because she had made the same trip the previous year, when she was a YTS trainee. However, the message is misunderstood by the retail trainees, whose common experience leads them to interpret 'station' as meaning 'bus station'. The message is sent and received; there is apparent agreement. No queries are raised, yet the misunderstanding concealed by apparent agreement results in chaos. The trainees miss their educational day trip to London and the parents and employees are angered by the apparent incompetence at County Hall (exacerbated by Marion omitting to send the explanatory letter). They complain to the Manpower Services Commission, which must investigate such apparent incompetence. This, combined with other criticisms outlined in this case, puts the validation of the Rutland YTS in jeopardy.

The second example of apparent agreement concerns the spoken word. Tracey Smith, the YTS trainee, has transcribed an audio tape containing an order for 'three gross of biro pens'. Her boss thinks that he is being explicit when he defines 'gross' for her, but in fact this causes confusion. Tracey believes that the figure 144 means the sum of three gross. Once again, a message has been sent and received with apparent agreement, but the misunderstanding which underlies this apparent agreement has repercussions for the company, the trainee, and the YTS. The company misses a bargain offer which would have supplied them with biros for a year, the trainee stands in danger of losing her job, and the scheme coordinator angers the manager when she defends the trainee. By exposing his fault in the matter, she provokes him into retaliating by making a complaint to the Manpower Services Commission.

Deliberate miscommunication

Once again, we have an example of apparent agreement over the guarantee on Helen Harcombe's car. Yet, the auctioneer's apparent agreement with Helen conceals ambiguity which is in fact an example of deliberate miscommunication. When Helen queries the words of the guarantee with him, he merely repeats what is written, thereby confirming that money will be refunded in twenty-four hours. By failing to point out that this actually means 'within twenty-four hours of purchase' he is guilty of misleading by omission. This shows apparent written and verbal agreement. It could well be argued that both parties are guilty of deliberate miscommunication and misunderstanding. The auctioneer misleads because he wants to make a sale, and the customer accepts the somewhat ambiguous written guarantee because she wants to believe that 'twenty-four hours' really means 'within twenty-four hours of complaining'. Notice, however, she never presses the auctioneer for clarification, merely confirmation of the written word. Her belief that her interpretation will be upheld in law, supports this view.

Cultural differences – same word, different meaning

'*Two great nations separated by the barrier of a common language*' George Bernard Shaw.

Here we have a misunderstanding over the definition of the word *broads*, The American mother believes that her son is about to be taken on a visit to some English ladies of doubtful reputation. The YTS organizer assumes that everyone knows what the Norfolk Broads are – an area of great natural and scenic beauty. The end result is that there appears to be a disagreement over the mother's support for an educational visit. This is far from correct. She would allow her son to go on an educational visit, but not one which apparently offers sex education. The whole conversation reveals two people talking at cross-purposes. It results in the mother becoming so angry that she threatens to report the organizers of the scheme to the Manpower Services Commission. The moral rectitude of the scheme has now been called into doubt.

It is important to note how much Marion Lane's preoccupation with her impending holiday affects the outcome of this conversation.

Failure to communicate

Marion Lane twice fails to communicate. The first instance, chronologically, is when she fails to let the liaison officer at the Manpower Services Commission know the dates of her holiday. The second is when she fails to send the letter, explaining the facts of the missed trip to the parents and employees of the retail trainees. Therefore the misunderstanding which results from this is compounded by two errors of omission.

The above incidents of miscommunication and failure to communicate, taken individually, are not potentially disastrous. However, their cumulative effect on the Rutland County Council's Youth Training Scheme threatens its future validation by the Manpower Services Commission.

Teaching guide summary

Issues	*Learning points*
1 The communication process.	• Key components.
	• Objectives of sender: intended message intended outcome.
	• Effects on receiver: perceived message actual outcome.
	• Use of appropriate channels: formal and informal written and verbal.
	• The need for feedback.
2 Miscommunication.	• Semantic differences.
	• Physical and mental distractions.
	• Cultural differences.
	• Apparent agreement.
	• Deliberate miscommunication.
	• Trust and openness.
	• Absence of feedback.
	• Defensive communication.
	• Interpersonal perception and attributes.

Teaching style

Have flip charts for each group, and white boards/black boards available for the lecturer to summarize the presentations of the groups.

Ask the groups to identify the miscommunications which are taking place in the case, and write on flip charts the key findings of each group. Then ask the groups to present their key findings. After the groups have finished their presentations, relate their findings to the key teaching points on a separate board. Ask the groups to present examples of similar types of miscommunication which have taken place in their own organizations (or between the class itself and lecturer!).

In the closing summary of the case, highlight the importance of interpersonal and organizational communication as a key element in improving personal and organizational effectiveness.

PART TWO

Strategic Management

ELEVEN

The Syntax Corporation

ANDREW P. KAKABADSE

Part 2

At the first meeting of the board, the members decided they needed to identify their goals and purpose, and issue a clear mission statement to the other managers in the organization. This they easily achieved. They stated that they intended to work towards a broad based brief identifying those strategic and operational problems that were not being confronted by any individuals or teams within Syntax UK. Bryant responded positively to such a broad based mission statement. He, in turn, issued a memorandum to all managers and supervisors of Syntax UK, stating that he fully supported the UK management board in what it was attempting to do and expected others in the organization to do likewise.

The next few meetings, however, did not proceed satisfactorily. Although the members of the board spent many hours together, they achieved little. They seemed unable to decide what problems they should initially examine. Each of the members in their turn expressed dissatisfaction at the way the meetings were being handled. The situation became worse when Peters and Capella threatened to resign on the grounds that they were spending a disproportionate amount of time attending fruitless board meetings. In addition, all felt that Ashcroft and Hall were opposed to the board, and hence, all but two (McConnell and Taylor) saw their careers as being in danger. McConnell despaired; the team that was sold as solving the unsolvable problems, was falling apart before it even started. He felt his future in the company was dependent on the team performing successfully.

McConnell called an extraordinary meeting to discuss with the board how he felt about events to date. Most of the other members of the group indicated that they were dissatisfied with the manner in which they had been handling their affairs. Further, all of the team members perceived Hall as wishing to take control of the board as he, supposedly, saw it as a stepping stone to being identified as the 'guy who put the UK right' and hence promotion in the USA would naturally follow.

The team decided on the following actions:

• Persuade Andy Taylor to chair board meetings. He, more than the others, had shown sensitivity to handling group processes.

• Work towards implementing a profit improvement programme (PIP) throughout Syntax UK. At the half year budget, expenditure was shown to be greater than income. If successful, PIP would justify to all in the organization, the need for the UK management board. Further, acting on PIP would uncover the coordination and communication problems in the organization. It was decided that PIP would form the core task for the board in the foreseeable future.

• Keep a special watch on Hall and if necessary, use McConnell as the negotiating medium between Hall and the board.

To effectively implement PIP, the board members concluded that they would have to convince other senior and middle ranking managers in Syntax of the need for profit improvement. They agreed to invite the key thirty cost centre managers in the organization to a whole day meeting to both inform them of Syntax's financial position and also brainstorm ways and means of improving profit.

It was decided that the whole day meeting should be split into three parts:

1 An initial plenary session outlining the need for PIP based on current financial statements.
2 The thirty managers should then be split into three subgroup workshops – manufacturing, administration and sales and marketing – to explore ways of implementing PIP within those functions. Capella and McSweeney would act as workshop leaders for the manufacturing group; Taylor, Jones and McConnell leading the administrative group, and Peters and Carter for the sales and marketing group.
3 A final plenary session bringing together the various contributions in order to formulate an agreed strategy for PIP.

Profit improvement programme

The day's meeting was anything but successful, though the day began positively. All thirty managers attended the meeting. At the initial plenary, Carter competently and dynamically presented the need for PIP. Most of the audience seemed interested, asked questions and seemed keen to participate in the workshops. The total group was then subdivided into three, with the manufacturing, administration and sales and marketing managers each attending their respective workshops. The manufacturing and administration workshops were well managed; most of the participants made contributions and a number of useful ideas concerning cost cutting exercises were generated. A great deal depended on the sales and marketing workshop. The manufacturing and administration managers could, at best, only cut costs. It was up to sales and marketing to increase revenue.

Peters and Carter were seen as having poorly managed the sales and marketing workshop. It quickly became clear that they were ill prepared for the meeting – their sales and marketing data was either wrong or out of date. Consequently, Peters and Carter spent a substantial amount of time just talking to each other, quarrelling with each other in front of the other participants or outside the workshop attempting to find accurate data. The workshop participants became bored, confused, and some angry.

'Why waste all this time?' demanded one senior, influential manager. 'Even when we offer you data, you don't listen,' he continued.

'How could PIP work with you guys?' questioned a second.

By this time, the other workshop participants had completed their task and wandered into the sales and marketing meeting. In full view of the other board members, Peters and Carter argued with each other, responded angrily to their workshop participants and seemed unable to control the meeting.

However, as the other workshops had drawn to a close, the sales and marketing meeting ended with one senior manager shouting: 'This has been a waste of time. Let's hear what the others have to say!'

The cost-cutting recommendations identified by the manufacturing and administration groups won the support of the plenary. Yet even with such savings, it became clear that Syntax would, at budget year end, be facing a £400,000 shortfall.

'You sales and marketing guys never get your act together! We make the sacrifices, can you get the sales?' growled Capella.

'Come on, you guys,' replied McConnell, 'we cannot fight like this in public.'

'Ok, I'm sorry!' replied Peters, 'I'm sorry sales and marketing did not perform well today. I promise you sales and marketing will have made up the £400,000 shortfall by budget year end.'

'How?'

'The sales and marketing group will meet and we'll find a way – that's how', responded Peters.

Shortly after, the meeting closed with a promise that the new sales strategy, to be developed by the sales and marketing group, would be documented and circulated to all present. On the closure of the meeting, McConnell called a Board Meeting. McConnell and Jones were furious.

'You two screwed it up!' Jones accused Peters and Carter. 'Why the hell fight in public?' shouted McConnell at Peters, Carter and Capella.

The accusations and counter accusations continued for another ten minutes. Finally McConnell asked the team members to stop fighting each other and concentrate on making positive contributions. The performance of Peters and Carter underwent close scrutiny. By now, Capella's frustration really showed – he threatened to resign. Peters also offered to resign, which Jones all too eagerly indicated he would accept.

'This team or board, or what the hell it is, is just a waste of time for me. I don't know what the hell we're supposed to be doing,' retorted Peters.

Peters continued to say that nobody really understood his job. '80 per cent of my time is spent selling products manufactured in the USA plants. Hence, revenue from my group's sales is credited to the USA. Only 10–12 per cent of my time is spent selling Syntax UK manufactured products,' exclaimed Peters.

'The UK entity needs more revenue. We are helping the Americans; they are not helping us; they may even close our manufacturing operation down!' exclaimed McConnell.

'That's not a big problem for me,' replied Peters calmly.

The others asked Peters to resign. He did so, pledged that he and his sales team would attempt to increase revenue for Syntax UK for this budget year, and then left the meeting.

Silence.

Then McSweeney, Taylor, Carter and McConnell stated they were upset with Peter's departure.

'We need him, even to represent the USA point of view', said McConnell.

'Look, ask him back,' stated McSweeney.

'No! If he comes back, I go, and I am part of the UK entity,' shouted Capella.

Various members of the board then accused each other of being insensitive, not caring and not contributing to the mission of the board.

'Look, this is a crisis!' stated McConnell. 'We can continue to fight each other, or do something about this', he continued. The others looked at each other, talked quietly to each other for a few minutes and then declared that they wished to function as a cohesive, integrated team.

McConnell stated that PIP could not be a success without Peters. He left the room to find him and invite him back to the meeting. Shortly, McConnell and Peters returned. Taylor suggested that the team should work towards developing a detailed strategy plan to effectively implement PIP; a task which they readily accepted. By the end of the meeting (1.30 a.m. the next day), it was assumed that Peters had rejoined the board, an assumption that Peters also held.

PIP was successfully implemented. Peters and Carter worked hard with the sales and marketing team to increase revenue. Despite a depressed market, they increased sales by £440,000 in that budget year. The rest of the board concentrated on the cost cutting exercises saving £150,000. Syntax UK showed a moderate profit.

Bryant publicly congratulated the board and stated he would continue to support its existence.

Ashcroft, until budget year end, had shown little interest in the board. He had grudgingly given tacit approval to his immediate subordinates – Jones, Carter and Peters – to sit on the board as long as their work performance did not deteriorate. He changed his view on seeing the PIP results. He too publicly supported the board.

Hall said nothing. He had for some time negotiated with Bryant to appoint him as Chairman of the Board. Bryant had considered that as the next logical step, should the board not perform as expected. The results of PIP altered Bryant's view. He did not wish to upset a successful team. Further, Bryant had considered developing 'self-regulating teams' for various activities. The UK management board proved to Bryant the value of self-regulating teams. Hall was told he would not be appointed as Chairman of the Board.

McConnell and Capella had been expecting some sort of response from Hall, four weeks passed and Hall made no comment verbally or on paper. Hall's silence worried the board members. Pressed by Carter, McConnell asked Bryant if he would meet the board to discuss its future. Bryant agreed.

The meeting with Bryant

'Just for the UK, it makes sense for Syntax and for the future role of the board, that PIP continue as an annual event,' said McConnell.

'The second issue is that product planning and manufacture as they impact on the Yeovil and Taunton plants require rationalization. As you know, both plants are my responsibility; only twenty months ago, the survival of both was under question. We've turned things round, but I want even better results. You know there is no exclusive UK champion other than Hall on PST (product strategy team),' stated Capella.

'These are the two main issues. The others that we wish to draw to your attention are . . . ,' continued McConnell.

For Bryant, the two were enough. Although McConnell was in full verbal flight, Bryant had ceased to listen.

'Profitability is my responsibility; once ok, but not every damn year. And what about Hall? That guy Capella sure means to get there – he's effectively asking me to give him half of Hall's job and to have a seat on PST – just like that!' reflected Bryant.

McConnell continued to talk. Bryant was still not listening.

'He's got a point though. He wants the UK manufacturing entity to survive. Just by the nature of things, Hall cannot be fully committed to that', thought Bryant.

'Sorry to interrupt, but the first two points are enough,' cut in Bryant. 'You all really know what he (pointing to Capella) has asked for?'

Silence.

'Well, as a compromise, how about O'Sullivan sitting on the board?' enquired Bryant.

Taylor looked hard at Bryant. O'Sullivan was his boss. It was common knowledge that Taylor was doing his best to distance himself from O'Sullivan.

As the conversation continued, Bryant could not have expected the degree of opposition to his suggestion that O'Sullivan should become a board member. Capella and Taylor made most of the comments.

'He's untrustworthy!'

'He's split the board!'

'We've worked too hard and too long to get us working as a group. Anyone could disrupt the works, no matter who he is!'

A lively debate developed. Nothing was decided except that Bryant would quickly communicate his decision. The board meeting finished.

Within three days, Bryant asked to see McConnell.

'Let me get to the point. PIP cannot be your full time responsibility. I've got to consider Hall and Ashcroft especially. What Capella wanted is out of the question, especially when you won't compromise on O'Sullivan,' stated Bryant.

McConnell showed no reaction.

'There is, however, one fundamental problem that requires attention – the whole people development question within the company within the UK. The truth is, we've not planned any training or development for our people. We spend crazy money on sending people on courses and don't know why we do it,' stated Bryant. 'Another thing, the board needs more stability. Having Taylor chair meetings isn't good enough. I want you as Chairman of the Board, reporting direct to me. That's the way to link my needs with the board's needs. What d'you think? Can it be done?' asked Bryant.

McConnéll was taken by surprise. He had not expected to drop PIP, but half expected Capella's bid for increased responsibility to be turned down. As for being full time Chairman of the Board, that was completely unexpected.

The two spent the rest of the morning and lunch, talking. Both agreed that the other board members would probably be hostile to their future non-involvement in PIP, but would welcome the opportunity to plan and develop the people side of the business.

'Me as Chairman? I just don't know how they are going to react to that', commented McConnell finishing his coffee at the end of a hard talking, working lunch.

The leadership of the board

McConnell had recognized that his appointment as Chairman of the Board could be viewed with suspicion. He concluded that he had to be elected; openly elected to allay any fears among the other board members.

'It's dropping PIP that could be the problem. Need to get them working on the people development programme (PDP) as soon as possible,' thought McConnell. He continued thinking, 'Also, now that Jones has got himself a job with another company, I'll get someone like Tim Stevens to take his place. I'll talk to him. He'll be ok.'

McConnell decided to talk to Capella, Carter and Taylor. A few days later, McConnell approached Capella.

'I heard about Bryant's change of game plan. That really upset me,' said Capella. 'Thought we had done a good job.'

'Probably PIP is central to Bryant. But, y'know, there is no one to impact the people side. Really depends on how you feel. Could be an opportunity. Bryant's already said he'd support you in the future,' commented McConnell.

He allowed Capella to talk. 'Just let him get all the negatives out,' thought McConnell.

The conversation continued for at least another hour.

For the last ten minutes, the two had been discussing the problems faced by the UK entity. It was Capella who suggested that the UK organization required its own champion.

'It's difficult to say that the UK needs its own Managing Director. The way we produce and sell our products: Peters sells most of the Sacramento products and some from Boulder, Colorado. For me, only some, and even then too few, are sold in the USA and have nothing to do with our marketing and sales boys. The rest, by a variety of means, are sold in Europe, the Comecon region and the Middle East. Doesn't need an overall top manager, but at least someone who can oversee operations'.

'Would also help if the board now had a proper and responsible chairman and . . . ,' McConnell couldn't finish his sentence.

'And you'd like to do that, yeh?' interjected Capella grinning.

Capella seemed to expect the suggestion, although he did present certain objections; would McConnell upset the team by trying to grab too much power; did McConnell have the personal skills to handle the job; could anyone handle the job – chairman of a Board – with no formal authority acting as an internal consultant/problem solver?

These issues were talked through; Capella soon agreed that McConnell was the man for the job.

To McConnell's surprise, Carter was even more supportive than Capella. 'Board needs to be stabilized to survive. The only one who can do it properly, because it's already part of his job is you, especially now that Bryant's proposed PDP – and that's a change of direction!'

Carter noticed McConnell's look of surprise.

'Of course I know. We all know. You can't keep anything quiet in this place', smiled Carter.

'Does that mean Capella knew all along?' enquired McConnell.

'Yeh. I thought I was giving him hot news. Bastard knew before I did!' smiled Carter, even more broadly than before.

McConnell felt annoyed that Capella had strung him along as he did.

The meeting with Carter soon finished with Carter pledging his support for McConnell.

Taylor was only too pleased to stop chairing board meetings. He indicated that he was not a good Chairman, felt he could not make the contribution on the board that he wished, and, in any case, had too many problems with his boss, O'Sullivan, to spend his time administering for the needs of the board.

That evening, McConnell reflected on the day's events.

'Can't say for sure, but it sounds like Hall. He's probably been pressurizing Bryant to do something about the board; probably about me too – we've had more downs than ups. Wouldn't be surprised if he then told Capella, just to let us know that nothing can take place without his knowing or being able to influence it. Hell, forget him. I'll go ahead with the agenda and one of the items will be my election as Chairman.'

McConnell in the chair

The next board meeting was a memorable occasion. First of all, there were nineteen items on the agenda and all nineteen items were discussed and actions identified.

Second, the election of McConnell took exactly twenty-seven seconds; all supported the motion and little was said. McConnell took the chair and went on to the next agenda items.

Third, Stevens was formally welcomed on to the board. Although some of his comments were misplaced at his first meeting, he neverthless made a valuable contribution. Most of all, he successfully attempted to become an integrated member of the team. The other members appreciated his efforts. No one indicated that they felt discomfort with a new boy on the scene.

A number of issues faced the board. First, the Marlborough site was to be sold off; some of the staff to be made redundant; some redeployed at the Yeovil and Taunton sites and others to join the new owners. Second, new canteen facilities were identified as being required at Taunton. Third, McConnell introduced the issue of working towards a unified, all embracing policy of staff training and development. Fourth, Peters proposed that the present annual appraisal forms – performance annual review (PAR) – should be reviewed and updated. From the ensuing debate, a programme of activities was identified, agreed to and actioned.

The board continued to meet at regular intervals over the next ten months, but more for the purpose of keeping colleagues updated on developments within their functional and board areas of responsibility. Some meetings were more fruitful than others.

A year later, the results of the combined endeavours was impressive:

1   The Marlborough site was sold with a lower than expected number of redundancies. Most employees wished to stay with Syntax. McConnell, together with Capella and Stevens, had negotiated mutually acceptable (to both employers and

employees) redundancy and redeployment agreements. The most powerful union in the company, ASTMS, gave management its support.

2 The board decided not to re-equip the existing canteen at Taunton, but build a separate dining and recreational facility. Within that year, the building was complete and required only a further three months' work in terms of installing equipment and fixtures and additional decorations before it could be fully utilized by the staff. Although a somewhat costly programme, Bryant, Hall and Ashcroft gave the board their full support as they considered that the money had been well spent.

3 McConnell produced an updated version of the PAR document. The cost centre managers and their subordinates considered the latest PAR a substantial improvement on the previous form. Although McConnell had made little headway with the staff training and development project, at least PAR contributed some way to the people development issue identified by Bryant.

Bryant was especially pleased with such results for two reasons. First, he had expected trouble with the closing of the Marlborough site and the ensuing redundancies and redeployment. Unknown to the board members, Bryant was told by the general manager, MLD, that if there was any further trouble with the UK products, in terms of quality of goods and meeting deadlines, the sites in the UK would be closed down and the same products manufactured at a new plant, running under capacity in Phoenix, Arizona. Bryant argued strongly that the only problem with the UK manufactured products was that the PST was constantly changing Hall and McSweeney's brief, which meant that Capella could never effectively plan his production runs. Further, Bryant felt that the UK operation was just being used as a scapegoat for certain manufacturing problems in Culver City and that Phoenix was running to under capacity as a result of Culver City's inefficiency. To no avail. What made it worse, was that the general manager was an Englishman. He could not even be accused of being partisan. The smooth closure of the Marlborough site was a relief to Bryant.

For the second time, Bryant publicly congratulated the work of the board. Hall wrote a short article on the board's 'splendid achievements' in the monthly newsletter. Ashcroft, now in Japan, sent to each of the board members a letter of congratulations, with special praise reserved for McConnell. Hall published the letter from Ashcroft to McConnell, in the newsletter. O'Sullivan made no public statement, but invited the board members out to dinner.

Questions

Please discuss the following questions in your study group and prepare a response for presentation in the plenary session;

1 How well has the UK Management Board managed its problems and challenges?
2 Could it have managed its problems better? If so, how?
3 Is the UK Management Board likely to function effectively? If yes, what sort of problems is it likely to face?
4 From your discussions, would you wish to make any changes to the criteria for effective team performance you identified in Part 1?

Part 3

It is now nine weeks since Bryant made his second public statement congratulating the board.

Ashcroft, for the last seven months, has really been operating from Japan. Three weeks ago, he announced that he would be operating full-time from Syntax head office, Nagoya, Honshu Island, Japan. Hall commented that Ashcroft now spent more time at Taunton, operating from Japan, than previously. However, Ashcroft has vacated his spacious Taunton office, now occupied by McConnell.

It was McSweeney who dropped the bombshell at the last board meeting five weeks ago. It happened at the customary report back, conducted at the beginning of all board meetings by each member, in order to update colleagues.

'One of the problems in completing board work has been the pressure in my own area on working on the 200 series; as you know, we are now well into model 203. David (Hall) wants the latest developments incorporated so that Tony (Capella) manufactures the product. Wants me to hire a couple more people to get things finished'.

Most of the board were only half listening. 'Boy, some meetings are boring', thought Carter.

'Probably hasn't got much more for next year. David seemed to think that the 203 would be the last version of the 200 series, or something like that', continued McSweeney.

'Fine. My turn', said Taylor sorting out the papers in front of him. 'As you know, grade 42 salaries are being reviewed, with the result that . . .'

'Hang fire! Hold on!' shouted McConnell, holding up his arm in

Taylor's direction. 'You've dropped a bombshell (pointing to McSweeney) or have I heard you right? There is nothing further planned after the 200 series? Is that right?'

McSweeney nodded tamely.

'What is there if there isn't the 200 series?' shouted McConnell.

'In a year's time, what happens to your people, and you want to take on some more now?' exclaimed Carter.

'Well, Tony was at the meeting with David. I'm afraid it's true,' shrugged McSweeney.

The significance of McSweeney's softly spoken statements hit home. The 200 series chemistry analyser was an innovative but small and simple instrument that could conduct numerous body fluids tests and give results within minutes. The 200 series had been considered the life blood of the Taunton site. The latest version (the 203) had proved to be so commercially successful that manufacturing was running at full capacity. In fact, all departments had had substantial involvement with the 200 series.

'What's going to happen if 203 goes?' asked Stevens (looking skywards).

'Will there be a UK entity?' questioned McConnell sarcastically.

The anxiety laden discussion continued. The reason for McSweeney's shy reticence and Capella's virtual non-contribution to the discussion was soon understood. Hall stated to his team that the information was absolutely confidential or else. . . . McSweeney considered himself the most vulnerable member of the team. If Hall did not provide him with further products to develop, what then? It would be up to Hall to redeploy him; which could be anywhere, and most probably in the USA, or if not that, then redundancy.

As the others were talking, McSweeney thought, 'Hell, if Hall finds out it was me, there's no USA, no job, no nothing. I'm out'.

After two hours of further conjecture, it was decided that McConnell and Carter should confront Hall on the basis that they had heard rumours flying around concerning the 200 series and would like them stopped before they got out of hand. All the board members promised McSweeney that nothing he had said would be related back to him. Taylor tried to make a joke out of the situation.

'Hello, David, confidentially-like, Robert tells us that the 200 series . . .' laughed Taylor.

No one else did.

Most board members commented after the meeting that, apart from anything else, Capella had been exceptionally quiet. All he seemed to have done was criticize Taylor for being late with two reports.

'Tony must feel the pressure as much as Robert', commented Stevens.

Hall, in fact, had been under pressure for some time. The American Presidents sitting on PST had been critical of the UK manufacturing entity in two ways, quality of product and costs. The view on PST was that Capella was too lax on quality control issues and that generally, the cost of manufacture in the UK was expensive. These issues had come to a head with the new plant in Phoenix, Arizona, running under capacity. The only factor in Hall's favour was that the skilled labour force required to manufacture the UK's product portfolio was concentrated in the UK. To transfer the manufacture of UK products to the USA would mean the transfer of existing personnel from the UK to the USA or the training of new personnel in the USA. The cost of both was considered prohibitive.

However, as a result of the pressure on PST, Hall committed himself to addressing the quality of manufacture problem. Hall knew he had to get closer to the Yeovil plant. Up to now, he had been based in London. Within a month of returning from the last PST meeting, Hall would move house, family and office to Yeovil. The most spacious and luxurious office in the Yeovil plant was Capella's. After initial discussions with Capella, Capella moved out of that office into a smaller one and Hall moved into Capella's old office.

For the next two months, Hall, Capella and McSweeney held a number of meetings and set short-term objectives in order to improve quality and also productivity.

Late one afternoon, McConnell received a telephone call from Hall. He asked that the two meet early that evening, to which McConnell agreed.

'Hi, Murray. Look, I've got a problem . . .', said Hall. He continued to explain how dissatisfied he had become with McSweeney. The man was not proactive; he was not firm enough with his own staff and was seen as weak by his American counterparts. The net result was that fewer and fewer projects were being issued to the UK for product development.

'That's not just because of the problems I've got on PST. It's more that the Americans don't respect McSweeney. The point is, I agree with them. I've come to the conclusion that he's got to go,' finished Hall.

McConnell had never liked Hall. He thought him arrogant, pompous and insensitive. However, McConnell had always respected Hall's abilities. In a strange way, McConnell felt satisfaction at being consulted over the McSweeney issue. What's more, McConnell knew that Hall had accurately summed up McSweeney. All the faults Hall outlined had been spotted by the members of the UK Management Board.

'If that's the way you feel, then McSweeney has to be made redundant', commented McConnell. McConnell thought for a minute, 'Let's make sure he is favourably treated! He has contributed in many ways'.

Within a month, McSweeney had left Syntax UK with a favourable redundancy package that Hall had negotiated with McConnell.

A month later, Hall rang McConnell once more, requesting another meeting.

'It's Capella', murmured Hall. 'We've more or less worked out how to handle the quality problems. It's just that I'm virtually doing his job as well as acting as a general manager for Yeovil. He hasn't got a job to do any more'.

McConnell and Hall had met and discussed a number of Syntax UK's problems since that first meeting concering McSweeney. This latest development came as no surprise to McConnell. Capella was one of the less popular managers in Syntax. However, he was good. As Capella had argued, many of the problems faced by manufacturing were not of his making. The constant changes of plan on PST and Hall's inability to negotiate a settled product portfolio with the Americans, had been the source of the problems concerning quality of manufacture. Capella had never been allowed the luxury of a settled production run for each product group. However, whatever the background, Hall had become heavily involved in the quality issue and taken over large sections of Capella's job. In turn, McConnell was most conscious of cost control. Although PIP was not the board's responsibility, many Syntax employees identified PIP with the UK Board. To have an unproductive senior manager on the payroll and also a board member, could mean that the board would lose its hard-earned credibility in the eyes of other employees. Yet, on the other hand, the likely reaction to Capella's departure by the board members, would be negative and that would mean trouble.

McConnell said little. After a while, he commented, 'I think you're right. Capella's got to go! There's little point in trying to get you and Capella to work together.'

Within a month, Capella had left the company with favourable redundancy package that Hall had negotiated with McConnell.

Questions

Please discuss the following questions in your study group and prepare a response for presentation in the plenary session:

1 How is the UK Management Board likely to react to McSweeney's and Capella's departure?
2 How important would you consider loyalty to be an issue for the board members?
3 How are the board members likely to view McConnell from now on and what impact is this likely to have as far as the future of the board is concerned?
4 What future role is the board likely to play in Syntax UK?
5 Is it likely that the board members will buy McConnell another drink?

Part 4

The departure of Capella and McSweeney in such rapid succession shook the board. Essentially, the other board members liked McSweeney, but did not respect him as a manager. Capella was not a popular figure, but he was respected. However, as a result of the Capella and McSweeney departures, Hall was viewed with even greater suspicion than ever before.

Ironically, the greatest antipathy was directed against McConnell. The other board members felt he had colluded with Hall in the redundancy of Capella and McSweeney. If anything, because of the redundancy packages, he knew the details of both cases, but seemingly offered little support to his two board colleagues. Carter and Peters attended meetings irregularly and when at meetings, made fewer and fewer contributions. Four months ago, Stevens had been transferred to manufacturing. He saw first hand, the problems in manufacturing and appreciated why Hall made Capella and McSweeney redundant. Stevens supported Hall and McConnell at board meetings. The relationships among the board members seemed to deteriorate.

Despite the internal problems on the board, Bryant was genuinely pleased with the results of the board's endeavours. The PIP and PAR projects and the new training programmes were generally considered successful. Furthermore, the board members had generally laid the groundwork for these to be ongoing programmes run by more junior managers. The successful closure of the Marlborough site and the rise in staff morale due to the improved canteen facilities were, in Bryant's eyes, attributable to the successful performance of the board. Bryant had also come to recognize another successful element of the board's contribution, which was not generally appreciated in the company. Historically, Ashcroft had acted as general manager

(GM) for Taunton, and Hall as GM for Yeovil, although neither of them had been given such specific responsibilities. With Hall giving greater attention to Syntax's manufacturing problems and Ashcroft's move to Japan, the two sites were more or less left managerless. The board had stepped in and probably had not even recognized, that they fulfilled the roles of GM at Taunton and Yeovil. As a result, the relationship between the managers of the two sites improved. The problems of the manufacturing managers were better appreciated by the marketing, sales and accounts managers, and vice-versa. Informal working groups were being set up to examine particular coordination problems between functions and between the two sites.

Yet, despite the board's contribution to the management of the Yeovil and Taunton sites, it was clear to Bryant that a general manager was needed for each site. Apart from anything else, the two sites were specializing in different activities. Yeovil concentrated on the manufacture of British products for distribution to marketing/ sales outlets throughout Syntax worldwide. Only a small percentage of Yeovil's products were being sold through the Taunton marketing/sales group. Taunton was now far more concerned than ever with the sale of USA manufactured products.

First, Hall was appointed GM of Yeovil with special responsibilities for manufacture as Vice President of Production. Second, Bryant hired head hunters to find a suitable GM for Taunton, but who also had substantial marketing experience. Eventually, a suitable candidate was identified and appointed as GM Taunton and Director of Marketing Syntax UK. His name was Robin Whittaker.

With the appointment of the two GMs, the successful management of PIP and the training programmes now delegated to a lower level of management, McConnell considered that the board had fulfilled its purpose. McConnell's relationship with Peters and Carter was improving as the Capella/McSweeney saga fell into the distant past, so he was able to discuss with them the 'winding up' of the board's activities.

McConnell was rather startled to receive a call from Bryant asking him to attend a 'total quality' meeting of all Syntax Personnel Directors and Vice President in Culver City.

'What's total quality?' queried McConnell.

Apparently, the discussions on quality control at PST, which had led to Hall taking greater control of the Yeovil site, had now progressed to considerations of how to improve the quality of Syntax's operations in all functions throughout the world. The Americans were particularly impressed with Hall's quality improvements of the UK manufacturing entity. In fact, at one PST meeting, it was Hall who coined the phrase – total quality – to become the banner for all manner of improvements throughout Syntax.

McConnell attended the Personnel Director's and Vice Presidents meeting in Culver City. He was so taken by the concept of total quality, that he strongly pressed for a Syntax international training programme on total quality, and then individuals identified in each country to ensure the application of total quality throughout Syntax nationwide.

The meeting accepted these proposals. McConnell and two other American Personnel Vice Presidents were commissioned to find the right consultant to help set up the total quality training programmes. A good consultant was found relatively easily, and a five-day programme was established. Managers of all functions throughout Syntax worldwide were earmarked for attendance on the programme, run at a hotel in Culver City.

McConnell was appointed as the UK total quality champion. Bryant publicly congratulated McConnell and stated that the UK management board would now have a further challenge to which he knew they could respond positively.

McConnell recognized that he needed to discuss total quality with Hall and Whittaker. He made appointments to see them both.

Questions

Please discuss the following questions in your study group and prepare for presentation in the plenary session:

1   What are the likely reactions of the two GMs to the total quality programme?
2   Is the UK Management Board likely to identify with the total quality programme? If yes, what sorts of problems are they likely to encounter in identifying and implementing a total quality philosophy in the UK?

Part 5

Events to date

A number of total quality training programmes were organized to run in the UK. The vast majority of the participants (persons holding a managerial appointment) considered the programme to be highly successful. In fact, a number of the participants invited McConnell to examine their part of the organization and see what improvements could be introduced. Hall was an enthusiastic supporter of the total quality programme.

Whittaker, however, spoke against McConnell's interventions into various parts of the organization, although he publicly supported the programme. McConnell tried to meet with Whittaker to discuss total quality and its possible value to the Taunton site, but Whittaker never seemed to be available to meet him.

Peters and Carter initially spoke out against the total quality programme. However, McConnell persuaded Peters to attend the programme, who returned 'singing its praises'. Peters, in turn, persuaded Carter to attend, who returned equally enthusiastic about the concept. Both began to attend to certain poor performance issues in the marketing and sales areas. Whittaker told them both that he considered their actions as interference. Despite his objections, Peters and Carter persuaded Whittaker to allow them to continue, but on the understanding that McConnell would not be involved.

With a change of mood in Syntax UK, Peters and Carter pressed McConnell to call for more board meetings. McConnell gratefully responded and with the support of his colleagues, invited two managers from Yeovil (manufacturing) to become board members, to take the place of McSweeney and Capella.

In fact, all the board members supported the total quality programme. Over the next six months, the board members discussed different approaches to total quality, identified further problems in the organization which required attention and, in turn, the various board members championed solving the problems identified.

Whittaker complained, at one of Bryant's management meetings, that his authority as a GM was being undermined by the recent interventionist activities of the board. Bryant stated he could understand why Whittaker felt the way he did, but the board was making substantial headway on the quality issues facing Syntax UK. McConnell, who happened to be a member of Bryant's team meeting, indicated that he wished the relationship between Whittaker and the board to improve. He would welcome talking to Whittaker about the board, total quality, and to what extent the board could be of value to Whittaker. Whittaker agreed to meet with McConnell.

Over the next three months, Hall and McConnell worked hard to eliminate most of the remaining manufacturing problems at Yeovil. The standards of quality of manufacture of products at Yeovil had been recognized by most of senior management in Syntax USA. Utilizing Syntax UK's new improved image, Hall re-negotiated the return of the 200 series, in terms of development and manufacture, to Yeovil. In addition, the new range of thermometers earmarked for testing, development and manufacture at Phoenix were transferred to Yeovil. Phoenix management were not too concerned, as they had already three new product lines to prepare for manufacture. The reason for this expansion was the result of the combined efforts of the USA and UK's marketing groups in gaining increased sales from the potentially lucrative Arab Middle East market.

In response to this expansion, Hall and McConnell decided to purchase the under-utilized plant and warehousing facility owned by a company situated next door to Syntax on the Yeovil industrial estate. The new purchase was to be termed Yeovil 2.

Bryant once again publicly congratulated the board on their success with the total quality programme.

McConnell, excited and satisfied with recent developments in the UK, was earmarked as the total quality coordinator for Japan. McConnell also recognized that he was becoming more interested in the concept of total quality than just Syntax. McConnell wondered to what extent total quality could be applied in other organizations.

'I wonder if I can make it on my own, consulting on total quality?' he pondered.

Introduction

The case of the Syntax Corporation highlights the *interpersonal processes* involved in the development of a newly formed group of executives as they progress into becoming a more effective management team. In addition, the *leadership qualities* of the team manager and the *influence of other key executives* in the organization are identified as *motivating* and *inhibiting* factors to improvements in team performance.

Theory and background

The case identifies the *opportunities, problems, sensitivities,* and *approaches* for improving the performance of management teams.

In the literature, different perspectives are available as to what constitutes effective team performance. Cummings (1981) indicates that an analysis of group/team performance needs to take into account individual, group and organizational values, group dynamics, and group growth and development processes. Overall, the growth and social needs of group members are best satisfied in *participative, self-regulating groups*. Under such circumstances, groups function more effectively if the values and beliefs of the managers, or leaders of the group (Nightingale and Toulouse 1977; McGregor 1960) and the shared values of the total organisation (Kakabadse 1982) are *supportive* of the *shared values* of the group members. In terms of group dynamics, a number of factors have been identified which could *promote* or *upset* the *interactions* between group members, such as the effort required by individuals to achieve *positive interpersonal relationships* in the group (Hackman 1976); the *influence* of the *group leader* (Glisson 1978); *group compliance* (Janis 1972); the *tasks* the group has to undertake (Blumberg 1980; Comstock and Scott 1977); stable and unstable *work environments* (Duncan 1973), and the *capability* of group members to introduce *change* to their work environment (Weick 1979). In terms of the necessary attention to growth and development of group members, Cummings (1978) and Hrebiniak (1974) consider the *group leader* as the *key stimulus* to generate a learning climate within the group.

The practical approaches to team development are neatly outlined by Margerison and McCann (1985) who provide realistic and easy to apply steps on how to *lead a winning team*. However, depending on circumstances within the organization and company culture, team development does have its *limitations* (Boss and McConkie 1981), as is outlined in the case.

Key learning points

The case examines how one person, Murray McConnell, attempted to create an effective management team out of a group of individuals brought together to address particularly frustrating problems that had not been given due attention within the existing management structure. In order to solve these problems, the group had to develop from being a collection of individuals into a *high performing team*. The process of generating a team identity and high standards of team performance are considered to be determined by:

1   The pattern of *interactions* between the individuals in the group.
2   The leadership *qualities* of the group leader.
3   The *values, influence* and *support* of other key managers in the organization.

In addition, it is proposed that as group members develop in terms of interpersonal maturity and in problem solving skills, they progress through distinct stages as part of a cycle of development. The cycle is termed the *team development wheel* (Figure 1), originally identified by Tuckman (1964).

Throughout this teaching guide, the terms 'group' and 'team' are used. Group is used to denote a collection of individuals who are working towards becoming an effective team, in the sense of the team development wheel. Team denotes a shared identity and mission and is used once a group has reached stage 4 in the team development wheel (see Figure 1).

Finally, as Syntax is a five-part sequential case, the key learning points are outlined for each part, highlighting the patterns of team member interaction, leadership qualities and the influence of other key managers as elements of each stage of the team development wheel. The full team development wheel model is presented after the feedback for Syntax Part 5. See the section on teaching style for further information on how to present this case.

Syntax Part 1:   Discussion notes

Forming

At this initial stage, the members of the newly established group need to become *acquainted* with each other's *views, values, expectations* and *objectives*.

Pattern of member interactions.   People in the group may feel inhibited in being too open with each other. The pattern of interaction is likely to be *guarded in disclosing personal* or *work orientated information*, or even in offering opinions on certain issues. It is likely that the members of the group will be *watchful* of each other's behaviour and conversation.

Leadership.   The leader needs to be aware that the group members, in order to perform effectively as a unit, need to know *more about each other*. It would be incumbent on the leader to help the team members 'break down' the interpersonal barriers between each other in order that the professional strengths of each individual are recognized. In addition, pressure is likely to be placed on the group to meet *particular targets*. The group will be unable to function if the team members remain guarded with each other. It is worth noting that two of the reasons McConnell chose the six managers for the UK Board was the fact that they knew each other and shared similar concerns in terms of the organizational problems facing Syntax UK. By having a common base, the group could, that much quicker, go about their task.

Organizational influence.   The views of other key managers within the organization towards the newly formed group is an important consideration. At this early vulnerable stage, *lack of support* or *active opposition* could terminate the group's existence. The lack of involvement of Ashcroft, Hall and O'Sullivan as members of the UK board potentially presents difficulties for McConnell. First, McConnell is the only member of the team who holds similar managerial status to Ashcroft, Hall and O'Sullivan, so that at least one team member can talk on equal terms with other senior managers. Equally, McConnell could end up '*isolated*' from colleagues at his level of managerial authority. Second, as the other members of the team report to Hall, Ashcroft and O'Sullivan, the issue of *split loyalties* could prevent the team from generating a shared identity. It is important for the future progress of the UK board, to *generate shared norms and values*, thereby allowing its members to agree on basic common issues which provide a focus for the ensuing debate on future direction. Third, Bryant's delegative style could be a problem for McConnell, as Bryant may not intervene if McConnell faced opposition from Ashcroft, Hall or O'Sullivan, despite Bryant's initial support to the formation of the UK board.

The forming stage involves identifying the members of a work group and initiating a process of breaking down barriers and inhibitions between group members and between the group and other key managers in the organization.

Distribute the discussion notes for Part 1 to the students at the end of the discussion of Syntax Part 1.

Syntax Part 2: Discussion notes
Storming
Once the members of the group overcome the testing stage by becoming acquainted with each other's skills, personal capacity, attitudes, styles and views through undertaking particular group tasks, certain *differences of opinion* or even *infighting* may occur among the group members.
   Patterns of member interactions. Members of the group may identify with *different* methods of styles to working on tasks or achieving objectives. Identifying with particular approaches to work may induce friction in the group, as individuals hold different opinions as to the most effective way of operating. An ability to resolve the friction is likely to cause poor group performance and under extreme circumstances, the departure of one or more members of the team. With such negative feelings prevailing in the group, the *integration* of any new members would be difficult.
   Further, poor performance on the part of any one or more group members could exacerbate existing tensions. The group would *relatively quickly* need to show *success* in *performance* in order to overcome external criticisms and, within the team, feelings of lack of

confidence. Under such circumstances, individual members may over-react to the poor performance of colleagues. The reaction of Jones and Capella to Peters' and Carter's inadequate preparation and inability to control the workshop addressing PIP, is indicative of how negative reactions can easily arise between group members. Significantly, it was quickly recognized that the UK board required the presence of Peters and Carter, despite the fact that Peters' job did not really require him to address the UK's sales, marketing and manufacturing problems.

A further reason for tensions in the group may be due to *personality differences*. Although the conflict may initially be confined to two or three group members, the resulting interactions and tension may influence and upset the remaining members.

There seem to have been few such personality clashes among the members of the UK board. Once the problem over the workshops with PIP had been overcome, the members of the board achieved their targets on PIP, sold off the Marlborough site with fewer than expected redundancies, built separate dining and recreational facilities and McConnell, in particular, improved PAR.

Leadership. The leader's priorities are to ensure that the group successfully *attains task goals*, and that the *internal conflicts* that will inevitably arise among members, are *adequately addressed*. It is important that the group displays an ability to perform effectively, otherwise other managers in the organization are likely to question whether the continued existence of the team is necessary. McConnell recognized the danger of lack of success and quickly became sensitive to the demotivating effects, on the members of the UK board, of attending fruitless board meetings. Hence, the group quickly pursued PIP and despite the internal difficulties, was able to achieve its objectives. That success, coupled with the successful sale of the Marlborough site, the building of the new recreation facilities and the updated PAR document, produced the necessary positive responses from Hall, Ashcroft, Bryant and O'Sullivan.

In terms of the interpersonal relationships, McConnell recognized the potential tensions among group members. All the members of the board seemed to be *professionally competent* and *task orientated managers*. There seemed to be few tensions due to personality differences. Most problems arose from the poor performance of one or more members. However, as leader, what could McConnell do? It is important to recognize that respect and trust in the leader is earned in this group and not just imposed. Initially, a non-threatening figure like Taylor was asked to chair meetings, a task he disliked, which was soon recognized as inadequate in terms of the long-term leadership of the board. Bryant considered McConnell as the true leader, appointed him as Chairman and negotiated with him concerning the future direction of the board. In response, McConnell displayed the necessary sensitivity to the feelings of his colleagues, and counselled their opinion before the appointment was officially ratified. McConnell can be considered, at this stage, as having moulded a team identity and an image of competence throughout the organization.

Organizational influence. The views and influence of other key managers in the organization are an important consideration for a group experiencing the storming stage. The survival of the group can be determined by these influential outsiders. Two issues will sway the opinions of key outsiders – *team performance* and the *capacity to fit,* or at least not threaten, the cultural norms of the organization. Syntax UK can be described as a *task performance* orientated culture with an *individualistic nature,* whereby managers are *expected* to *negotiate* with others in order to achieve their objectives. *People earn their rewards.* Role and status does not automatically provide the individual with an advantage. As far as performance is concerned, the UK board's achievement with PIP was widely acclaimed, except by Hall. Hall wanted control over the board, but felt he was losing advantage in his influencing of Bryant, because of the board's performance. Hall was not ready to acknowledge the board's performance.

Similarly to Hall, the board members recognized the value of negotiation within Syntax's rather individualistic, assertive culture. The UK board's meeting with Bryant, through which they unsuccessfully attempted to improve the status of the team by attaining representation on PST, but their successful blocking of O'Sullivan becoming a board member, is indicative of the growing confidence of the board and their need to make an impact on the organization. Finally, however, the performance of the team (Marlborough site, PAR etc.) positively swayed the opinion of key managers in favour of the team.

The storming stage is epitomized by tensions and conflicts in the group, due to performance, leadership, long-term direction, and personality reasons, coming to the surface.

Distribute the discussion notes for Part 2 to the students at the end of the discussion of Syntax Part 2.

Syntax Part 3:   Discussion notes

Norming

The group may quickly progress through storming stage, or may experience considerable tensions and difficulties in the relationships between group members. However, sooner or later, the group is likely to mature to the norming stage, whereby meaningful and shared norms of behaviour and professional practice begin to be established.

Pattern of member interactions.   The interpersonal barriers between group members begin to *dissipate* as a result of individuals exchanging views, ideas and experiences on professionally related problems. The understanding between the group members, as shown towards the end of Syntax Part 2, would typify a more mature pattern of group interaction.

Leadership.   Breaking out of the storming stage substantially depends on the *skills of the leader*. Through achieving particular work results, the leader needs to develop the skills of giving feedback, listening, confronting issues, and thereby establishing professional trust and rapport between himself and group members.

Organizational influence.   Achieving task goals successfully and in a manner acceptable to the cultural norms within the organization, is likely to generate support from other key managers in the organization.

Norming is epitomized by generating a sense of shared identity and meaningful future direction among group members.

Norming/storming cycle

Despite progress on task and group identity issues, the group may *regress* to stage two (storming) and *fluctuate* between stages two and three. Such regression can occur for three reasons; individual members, especially new members, may *challenge* certain newly formed practices, procedures or group norms; the group leader may behave in a manner which other members find *unacceptable*, and hence he *loses their trust*; the sudden and/or unexpected *departure* of one or more key members.

The change of fortune of the Development and Manufacturing Group, over the 200 series, led to the latter two processes. The board's inability to confront Hall over the future of the 200 series and the pressures on Hall to re-examine the UK product portfolio and the quality of the UK manufacturing process, led to the departure of the two weaker members of Hall's group who were prominent members of the board. However, Hall treated McConnell as a colleague of professionally equal standing, in terms of solving sensitive personnel problems. McConnell responded equally maturely and, under the circumstances, could see little alternative, other than the departure of McSweeney and Capella. McConnell's main anxiety was the reaction of his own board colleagues. Naturally so, for the team had developed its own values and identity which may *not have matched* with the *expectations* of other key managers in the organization. Under such circumstances, the person most vulnerable is the leader of the team who cannot afford to be seen to *undermine* the expectations of his team members and yet has to *positively respond* to *organizational demands* in order to maintain his *credibility* in the organization and *enhance* the *image* of the team.

Distribute the discussion notes for Part 3 to the students at the end of the discussion to Syntax Part 3.

Syntax Part 4:   *Discussion notes*

Breaking out of the storming/norming cycle
Breaking out of the storming/norming cycle is no easy matter. A great deal will depend on the *attitudes* of the group members, the *skills* of the leader and the *actions* of other key managers in the organization.

Pattern of member interaction.   The group members are likely to feel *demotivated* and *unable* to *focus* or *commit* themselves to the group task(s). Tensions and conflict may emerge between group members and/or attendance at meetings and commitment to action may be low. The leader, rightly or wrongly, *may be blamed* for the problems facing the group, as was McConnell. After Capella and McSweeney's departure, members of the board attended fewer meetings, and performance for a while seemed to deteriorate. However, in order to break out of the storming/norming cycle, the group members need to identify with a common identity or so as to rebuild relationships and provide a task focus.

Leadership.   A great deal depends on the *skills* of the group leader both to assist the group members to identify with each other by *openly confronting* the problem issues, and to find sufficiently *challenging* tasks that would demand a team approach to problem solving and thereby unite the group members. For McConnell, the total quality programme could provide the necessary focus he needs to motivate the group members.

Organizational influence.   The *attitude* and *behaviour* of key managers toward the group is a crucial factor as to whether the team breaks out of the storming/norming cycle or whether its performance gradually deteriorates. If the group faces opposition or poor cooperation from other managers in the organization, the members are poorly motivated to generate a meaningful strategy to address such negative influences. Bryant was the most supportive, for he recognized the contribution of the group. However with Ashcroft's departure and the appointment of the two GMs, the attitude of two out of three key managers could determine whether the group would continue to function or cease to operate.

Breaking out of the storming/norming cycle depends on the group members or the leader establishing a workable common ground so as to rebuild the relationships within the group.

Distribute the discussion notes for Part 4 to the students at the end of the discussion to Syntax Part 4.

Syntax Part 5:   Discussion notes

Performing

In order for the group to break out of the storming/norming cycle, it must identify with a meaningful mission or purpose which will provide a greater sense of identity among its members.

Pattern of member interactions. A *meaningful sense of purpose* may emerge from the debates and discussions that took place during the storming/norming phase. Group members should be more *supportive* of each other, sharing information and ideas, and tolerating each other's differences. In addition, a more *mature sense of professionalism* begins to emerge. The tasks and issues facing the group are addressed despite the interpersonal sensitivities among its members. It is unlikely that the interpersonal tensions will disappear, but more that *meeting group objectives will be given priority.*

The change of attitude of Peters and Carter, towards the board and McConnell, after attending the total quality programme, greatly assisted the group to enter into the performing stage. Peters and Carter pressed for more board meetings. Peters and Carter persuaded Whittaker to allow them to apply the total quality concept in the marketing and sales areas, as long as McConnell was not to be involved. In fact, all the board members championed various projects in Syntax, including McConnell, who together with Hall, attempted to eliminate the manufacturing problems at Yeovil.

Groups that enter into the performing stage, utilize each other's strengths and talents to a greater degree. The group is now at its most resourceful and flexible in its approach to problem solving and task performance. In fact, the group has developed into an effectively performing team.

Leadership. In order for the group to break out of the norming/storming cycle, the leader would have had to effectively apply *interpersonal, counselling* and *listening* skills in order to be able to facilitate reconciliation between warring members, and to provide new direction in terms of group goals. Having helped the group to attain task competence and supportive interpersonal relations, the leader then needs to adopt a lower profile. The leader has contributed to the process of turning a group into a team. Team members should have the confidence to work on new tasks and challenges and to effectively utilize each other to achieve agreed objectives. To competently address task challenges, individual members require sufficient independence in order to take initiative and display their professional skills. To be perceived as providing too much direction could demotivate team members. The leader would need to intervene only if difficulties or tensions arise in the team, or when periodically reviewing the future direction the team should take. The leader is likely to adopt the role of counsellor, providing help and support to individual members when appropriate. McConnell, through the total quality programme, was able to provide the impetus for pursuing meaningful and challenging team goals. However, in his behaviour he acted as one more resource that the UK board offered Syntax, concentrating on attending to the quality problems facing Hall.

Organisational influence. Once the group has matured and attained the performing stage, the views, values and behaviour of other key managers in the organization, are *less likely to be perceived as a threat.* In fact, *criticism* and *opposition* to the team are more than likely to be seen as a *challenge requiring attention.* McConnell's positive response to Whittaker's criticisms, and his partnership with Hall in eliminating the manufacturing problems in Yeovil, indicate a self confidence in one's own and the team's ability to confront organizational problems.

As a result of utilizing each other's strengths and talents to a greater degree, the group is more resourceful and flexible in its approach to problem solving and task performance. The group has matured and is performing as an effective team.

The departure of key members of the team, as hinted by McConnell wishing to become a consultant, may induce the team to fall back into any one of the stages in the team development wheel. If the new members do not integrate well, then the team could well find itself back at the forming stage. Equally, substantial changes of direction, objectives or mission may well force the team to re-think the manner in which it conducts its work and the skills required of its members. Hence, new members may be required, and then the team may regress to stages 3, 2 or 1 in the team development wheel. Finally, changes of longer term strategy in the organization may lead to the disbandment of the existing team and the formation of a new one. The new group would enter into stage 1 of the team development wheel.

Distribute the discussion notes for Part 5 to the students at the end of the discussion to Syntax Part 5.

Teaching guide summary

Issues
Forming

Learning points

1 Pattern of member interactions.

- Becoming acquainted with the views and values of other members.

2 Leadership.

- Break down interpersonal barriers.
- Focus on task/group objectives.

3 Organizational influence.

- Opinions and behaviour of other key managers in the organization is vital.
- Split loyalties.

Storming

1 Pattern of group interactions.

- Infighting between group members.
- Differences of approach or style leads to tensions.
- Negative reaction to poor performance.
- Personality clashes.

2 Leadership.

- Help members to achieve group goals.
- Address interpersonal issues.
- Interpersonal skills to address sensitive issues.

3 Organizational influence.

- Survival of the group can be determined by influential 'other' managers.
- Support offered if group performance is high.

- Group should not deliberately threaten cultural norms of organization.
- Respected if group fits with culture.

Norming

1 Pattern of group interactions.

- Shared norms are identified.
- Breakdown of sensitive interpersonal barriers.
- Greater individual maturity and understanding of strengths/weaknesses of other members.

2 Leadership.

- Confronts sensitive interpersonal barriers.
- Effective utilization of interpersonal skills.
- Focus on group tasks.
- Utilize strengths of each team member.

3 Organizational influence.

- Overall support of group is culturally acceptable.

Norming/storming cycle

- Splits and tensions occur in group.
- Vulnerability of group leader due to conflicting demands.
- Departure of key members.
- Performance of group deteriorates.
- Group lowly motivated to face opposition from other key managers.

Breaking norming/storming cycle

- Re-establish shared norms in order to increase performance.

1 Pattern of group interaction.

- Group members likely to be demotivated.
- Low commitment to action.
- Need focus in order to motivate group members.

2 Leadership.	• Group leader to provide task focus.
	• Confronts interpersonal tensions.
3 Organizational influence.	• Support of other key managers is crucial in preventing collapse of group.

Performing

	• Effective performance due to generation of meaningful team mission.
	• Group has developed into a high performing team.
1 Pattern of member interaction.	• Team members tolerant of each other's differences.
	• Greater sharing of information.
	• Supportive in addressing task challenges.
	• Interpersonal tensions are secondary to professional performance.
	• Greater utilization of team members' strengths and talents.
2 Leadership.	• Low profile.
	• Intervenes to diffuse interpersonal tensions.
	• Effective application of interpersonal skills.
3 Organizational influence.	• Opposition to team less likely to be perceived as threat.
	• Positive response likely to problems arising within the team or in the organization.

This summary can be prepared for acetate or flip-chart presentation, and used for providing a comprehensive summary at the end of case discussion.

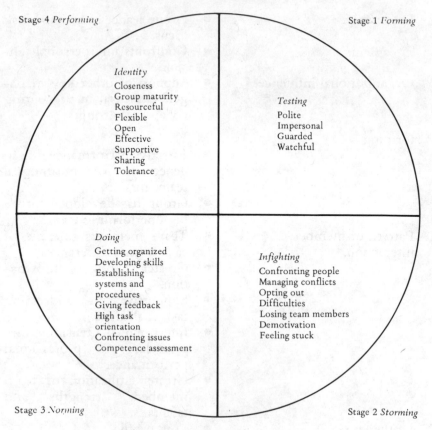

Stage 4 *Performing*　　　　　　　　　　　　　　　　　　　Stage 1 *Forming*

Identity
Closeness
Group maturity
Resourceful
Flexible
Open
Effective
Supportive
Sharing
Tolerance

Testing
Polite
Impersonal
Guarded
Watchful

Doing
Getting organized
Developing skills
Establishing
systems and
procedures
Giving feedback
High task
orientation
Confronting issues
Competence assessment

Infighting
Confronting people
Managing conflicts
Opting out
Difficulties
Losing team members
Demotivation
Feeling stuck

Stage 3 *Norming*　　　　　　　　　　　　　　　　　　　Stage 2 *Storming*

Figure 1　*Team development wheel*
(*Source*: B. W. Tuckman, 'Developmental sequence in small groups',
Psychological Bulletin, vol. 63, no. 6, 1965, pp. 384–99.)

Teaching style

This is a five-part sequential case and requires a four-hour period for
teaching. The participants should consider Part 1 and address
themselves to the three questions at the end of Part 1. Regroup the
participants in the plenary, and request views, ideas and evidence as
response to the questions. Take down the key points offered on flip
chart. Issue Part 1 discussion notes on completion of class
discussion. The discussion notes related to each part attempt to
summarize the issues addressed in the case and also to prepare the
students for the following case part. Issue Part 2 of the case for the

plenary to consider in their subgroups. Blutack the group's responses to Part 1 on the classroom wall. Repeat the process until all five parts of the case and appropriate feedback has been issued.

In the final summary of the case, draw to the group's attention their views as recorded on flip chart, and contrast them with the feedback notes to each case part. Emphasize the issues and problems of developing effective management teams.

Conclude the session by presenting on acetate, the teaching guide summary and Figure 1, the team development wheel, indicating that turning a group of individuals into an effective performing team requires skill, effort and considerable insight in order to accurately interpret the behaviour of team members or other executives in the organization. From there on, it is possible to act appropriately in order to match the stage of development of the group or the expectations of other key executives.

References

M. Blumberg, Job Switching in Autonomous Work Groups: An Exploratory Study in a Pennsylvania Coal Mine, *Academy of Management Journal*, vol. 23, 1980, pp. 287–306.

R. W. Boss, and H. L. McConkie, 'The Destructive Impact of a Positive Team Building Intervention', *Group and Organisation Studies*, vol. 6, 1981, pp. 45–66.

D. E. Comstock, and W. R. Scott, 'Technology and the Structure of Sub-Units: Distinguishing Individual and Work Group Effects,' *Administrative Science Quarterly*, vol. 22, 1977, pp. 625–34.

T. G. Cummings, 'Self-Regulating Work Groups: A Socio-technical synthesis', *Academy of Management Review*, vol. 3, 1978, pp. 625–34.

T. G. Cummings, 'Design Effective Work Groups', in Nystrom and Starbuck (Eds.) *Handbook of Organisational Design*, vol. 2, (Oxford University Press, 1981) pp. 250–71.

R. B. Duncan, 'Characteristics of Organisational Environments and Perceived Environmental Uncertainty', *Administrative Science Quarterly*, vol. 17, 1972, pp. 313–27.

C. A. Glisson, 'Dependence of Technological Routinisation on Structural Variables in Human Service Organisations', *Administrative Science Quarterly*, vol. 23, 1978, pp. 383–95.

J. R. Hackman, 'Group Influences on Individuals,' in Dunnette (Ed.) *Handbook of Individual and Organisational Psychology*, (Rand McNally, 1976) pp. 1455–1525.

L. G. Hrebriniak, 'Job Technology, Supervision and Work Group Structure,' *Administrative Science Quarterly*, vol. 19, 1974, pp. 395–410.

J. L. Janis, *Victims of Group Think* (Houghton–Mifflin, 1972).

A. P. Kakabadse, *Culture of the Social Services*, (Gower, 1982).

C. Margerison, and R. McCann, *How to Lead a Winning Team*, (MCB University Press, 1985).

D. McGregor, *The Human Side of Enterprise*, (McGraw-Hill, 1960).

D. V. Nightingale, and J. M. Toulouse, 'Toward a Multi-level Congruence Theory of Organisation,' *Administrative Science Quarterly*, vol. 22, 1979, pp. 264–80.

B. W. Tuckman, 'Development Sequences in Small Groups', *Psychological Bulletin*, vol. 63, no. 6, 1965, pp. 384–99.

K. E. Weik, *The Social Psychology of Organising*, 2nd ed., Addison-Wesley, 1979.

TWELVE

The Box Makers:
the case of SafePAC plc

ANDREW P. KAKABADSE

Introduction

The case of SafePAC plc focuses on the processes of strategy formation and implementation in organizations. The case highlights the inherent tensions that arise from the generation of corporate strategy and the manner in which it impacts on business unit strategy. The nature of these tensions and the way in which they can be addressed are the learning points to draw from the case.

Theory and background

The terms strategy and policy have been defined in a multiplicity of ways. Overall, strategy and policy are considered to be the means by which the mission of an organization is achieved. In effect, strategy is an intention which takes mission statements and long-term objectives and turns them into a meaningful series of plans of action.

Substantial differences of opinion exist in the literature as to the nature of the processes of strategy formation and decision making. On the one hand, strategic processes are interpreted from a normative standpoint, whereby all-embracing models are offered so that the making and integration of strategic decisions into the wider organizational context is both feasible and desirable. The emphasis is on a scientific approach to contingency forecasting in order to draft plans, designs and strategies which are comprehensive in nature. The early cybernetic interpretation of decision making of Cyert and March (1963) or Scott (1967) arose from applying decision making concepts, which held a strong economic perspective, to the behavioural sciences. Equally, the normative approach has been applied in the clinical area (Ingelfinger 1975; Lusted 1968), whereby the role of clinical judgement in diagnosing patients promotes the physician's scientific obligation to advance medical theory and practice. Meyer (1984) postulates that medical practitioners and health service administrators adopt the self-same model when involved in the purchase and evaluation of medical equipment and services. Hence, the normative school emphasizes the strategic formulation process as highly rational, involving activities such as establishing goals, monitoring environments, assessing internal capabilities, searching for and evaluating alternative actions and, as a result, developing an all-embracing strategic plan to achieve identified goals. (Particular references to pursue are Ansoff 1965, 1982; Grant and King 1979; Hoffer and Schendel 1978; Thompson and Strickland 1978; Perrow 1970; Galbraith 1977: Miles and Snow 1978.)

In complete contrast to normative thinking is the incrementalist approach (Fredrickson and Mitchell 1984) whereby strategic decision making is considered to be the result of countless loosely-linked planning decisions made over a period of time, but which at least adhere to a particular theme or trend. The trend may or may not be consciously recognized (Quinn 1980; Miller, DeVries and Toulouse 1982). Protagonists of the normative school, such as Mintzberg (1973; 1978), Mintzberg and Walters (1982), Lundblom (1979) argue that incrementalist thinking is a far more accurate reflection of how organizations really make strategic decisions. For example, Wildavsky (1968) suggests that the budgeting process is an opportunity for individuals to negotiate the allocation of financial resources. In this way, Wildavsky (1968) sees strategy and policy as an arena of conflict over whose preferences are to prevail in the determination of policy. Hofstede (1978) endorses the view by indicating that management control systems, such as PPBS and MBO are ineffective, as they are based on a cybernetic philosophy which is homeostatic in approach as opposed to organizational environments which are heterostatic in approach.

In this case, an incrementalist interpretation of strategy formation and implementation is adopted. The views, business values, demands and behaviours of key executives are considered important influences in the formation and application of strategy. It is also considered relevant to examine the different perspectives adopted by executives depending on the position they hold in the enterprise. Executives who are concerned with the long-term future of the business unit per se (see key learning points) may hold different views concerning profitability and business success to an executive representing a headquarters/corporate role (corporate strategy). Due to the differences of vision, values and beliefs held by each executive in a strategic decision making forum, the generation of strategy and its application is considered to be the outcome of continuous negotiation.

Key learning points

The case concentrates on the problems and challenges facing the board of SafePAC plc in general and their Chief Executive, Peter Girling, in particular. The following points need to be drawn to the students' attention during case discussion.

1   Business unit strategy *vs* corporate strategy.
2   Managerial values.
3   Consultant intervention.

Business unit strategy vs *corporate strategy*

Strategy is an all-embracing term. For it to hold specific meaning, it is necessary to distinguish between different types of strategy, which in the case are identified as business unit and corporate strategy.

Business unit strategy is adopted by business units, which are identifiable, single-product (or related multi-product) organizations such as independent companies, subsidiaries, or a division of a corporation. The essential feature of a business unit is that the organization is identified with a single range of products or services so that its mission is singularly clear. The success or failure of any organization depends on the performance of the business units. The performance of the business units is influenced by their overall philosophy, organization structure, attitudes of employees, product portfolio, competitive position in the market and sensitivity to changes in the market place.

In contrast, corporate strategy relates to organizations which control a number of business units such as multi-nationals or multi-purpose local government organizations, as in the UK. The aim of corporate strategy is to stimulate a corporate identity among the different business units, help improve the performance of the business units and be sensitive to developments in the market place so as to be able to focus on new areas of business activity. Hence, the issues underlying corporate strategy would be the spread of business areas and whether conflicts of interest exist between the business units. Further, the concept of strategic thrust is crucial, i.e. in which areas are future strategies to be concentrated – within existing business units, or have new areas of business been identified – and how has capital assistance been distributed among the units?

Whereas business unit strategy is geared towards achieving business results, such as profitability, effective provision of services or reducing costs, corporate strategies do not directly share such aims. Effective corporate strategy has as its objective the survival of the corporation as an entity, through the increased performance of the business units; through identifying new areas of business or through allocating and re-allocating capital assistance to the business units.

Explore the conflict of interest between SafePAC and the parent company. SafePAC is operating in a declining industry whose operating surplus is reduced by the area head count tax and a contribution to venture capital for other corporate ventures. Further, SafePAC is being pressurized to reduce operating costs, the true reason for the closure of the Chesterfield plant. Examine with the group, the pressures, constraints and opportunities faced by Girling as the person who represents corporate and business unit strategy, to two different boards of directors. Through an opportunities, pressures and constraints analysis, highlight the sort of working relationship Girling has developed with the members of the SafePAC board and the implications in business terms of having negotiated such relationships. Discussion on the quality of executive working relationships and the impact such relationships have on the business, provides a good introduction to the discussion on managerial values.

Managerial values

The case indicates that the profitability and growth of a business enterprise is dependent on the effective performance of one or more senior management teams, which for the Box Makers is the board of the subsidiary SafePAC. It is highlighted that effective team performance is strongly influenced by the interactions and relationships of the executives within the team. Such interactions are, in turn, largely determined by the vision, values and beliefs held by each executive about the future direction of the business and its management in the most effective manner. Executives do feel strongly about what is happening in their business and the strategies that they should adopt for the future. Two sets of values emerge from the case; the future direction of SafePAC; the manner in which the organization is managed. The conflict of interests between the demands of the corporate board and the best interests of SafePAC place Girling in a difficult position. The closure of the Chesterfield plant is likely, in the long run, to benefit corporate headquarters rather than SafePAC. The head count levy is partially a mechanism for raising capital to support new corporate ventures such as the information technology company.

Such tensions have repercussions concerning the manner in which the organization is managed. The level of trust and commitment to agreed strategies is low on the SafePAC board. In attempting to apply corporate views to SafePAC, Girling is opposed by his own board. The Chesterfield plant issue highlights the behaviours that Girling needs to adopt in order to get policies through the board. His ability to reverse opposition by talking to his directors on a one-to-one basis was effective in terms of agreement to close the Chesterfield plant, but at the expense of the trust of the board members in their Chief Executive. Girling recognized the interpersonal problems on the board and called in a consultant to help improve the situation.

Understanding that some of the problems are due to the conflict of interests that the Chief Executive needs to manage, Girling also recognized deficiencies in terms of effective executive behaviour of his board colleagues. The position adopted by Harper is interesting to explore. Has he sided with the general managers? Does he find Girling too overpowering to work effectively with him? Certainly, Harper indicates little ownership of corporate strategy issues or with Girling and his problems. Girling needs to nurture his relationship with Harper, as the general managers report to Harper and they are the wealth creators for SafePAC. Whichever strategies Girling wishes to adopt, he needs the support and cooperation of the general managers, for they provide the interface between the company and its market.

Consultant intervention

With such differences of values between the board members, it is inevitable that little trust exists between them. The consultant should aim to increase the level of trust between them.

Towards this end, the approaches the consultant could adopt are:

1 Recommend that a workshop be organized. At the workshop, all board members would attempt to identify how performance on the board could improve. The consultant should act as facilitator and aim to stimulate an open discussion about the problems facing the board and the feelings of each individual member towards the company and its leadership. In this way, the different role demands, constraints and opportunities of each board

member could be brought out into the open. By a sharing of problems, greater understanding of each other's difficulties could take place, so that a more meaningful examination of alternative solutions could be undertaken by the board members.

2 Recommend further one-to-one meetings with each board member so as to discuss their perceptions of the problems and recommendations, with a view to providing data-feedback to the board. In this way, confidentiality concerning each individual's views could be maintained. The board could, with this information, focus on identifying solutions to their problems.

Approach 1 would involve more risk for the board as it depends on relatively free and open discussion between the board members. The state of relationships on the board could inhibit such conversation. Alternatively, the board members could unite and directly confront and attack Girling, thereby inhibiting the building of trust between the individuals. If strategy 1 were to be adopted, it would be incumbent on the consultant to work individually with each board member in order to prepare them for open discussion.

Approach 2 is a lower risk strategy as the consultant acts as an 'information filter', controlling the degree of adverse opinion and focusing attention on the need to find ways of improving the present situation.

If the student group generates further approaches, list them in addition to 1 and 2, and ask the plenary to list them in rank order, offering reasons as to the ranking.

The ultimate aim of the consultant, with whatever approach is adopted, is to assist each board member to understand the nature of the problems facing the group. Little progress can be made until the pressures facing Girling, by virtue of holding dual membership of the corporate and business unit boards, are appreciated by the others. Such insight is the first step to identifying with the chief executive, his policies and the constraints he needs to overcome.

In addition, the consultant needs to assist the board members to offer constructive feedback to Girling concerning his managerial style. The aim is to stimulate closer working relationships between Girling and his board colleagues. However, the board members will first need to inform Girling that his current behaviour pattern is affecting them adversely. The consultant should, in turn, aim to support Girling during this process. It would be a natural response by Girling to become defensive and either not listen or respond negatively to the comments of his colleagues.

If the process is sensitively managed, all parties can emerge positively from the encounter. The board members could indicate what more appropriate management style(s) should be practised by Girling in order to help improve their performance. Girling, in turn, could outline the difficulties in satisfying all the parties with whom he interacts due to the contraints in his role.

The process of talking through the various problems facing the SafePAC board will allow the board members to agree on what is effective behaviour on the board. Girling could indicate what he requires from his colleagues in order to appropriately address issues and thereby improve performance. The board members could indicate, from each other and from Girling, what is effective behaviour, in order that their problems can be understood and addressed. Emphasize to the students that competence at senior level is more dependent on being able to understand, negotiate and identify with coherent strategies concerning the business, than it is on professional skills.

Teaching guide summary

Issues	*Learning points*
1 Strategy.	• Business unit strategy is related to single mission organizations.
	• Success or failure depends on performance of business units.
	• Corporate strategy applies to organizations which control a number of business units.
	• Aim of corporate strategy is to stimulate corporate identity.
	• Potential conflict of interests between business unit *vs* corporate strategy.
2 Managerial values.	• Executives identify with particular values concerning the business.
	• These values influence the nature of interactions and relationships in management teams.
	• Differences of vision and values need to be addressed in order to improve team performance.
	• Trust between colleague executives is as much dependent on the shared/unshared values as it is on managerial style.

3 Consultant intervention.

- Executives discuss each other's constraints.
- Identify differences of values between them.
- Generate greater commitment to each other.
- Consultant as facilitator to stimulate personal feedback.
- Overcoming blockages is necessary in order to identify coherent strategies for the business.

This summary can be prepared for acetate or flip-chart presentation and used for providing a comprehensive summary at the end of case-discussion.

Teaching style

Make available a whiteboard or a flipchart with the facility to Blutack three or four flipchart sheets to a wall.

Ask the groups to present the results of their discussion of each question. After the groups have finished their presentations, fit their findings into the structure of the teaching guide on the whiteboard or separate flipchart sheet. As the key points of business unit *vs* corporate strategy, managerial values and consultant intervention are being presented, highlight these points to the class, encouraging discussion and explanation.

In the closing summary of the case, emphasize the importance of managerial values as a determinant of business success, stressing how differences of values arise at both the individual and organizational levels.

References

H. I. Ansoff, *Corporate Strategy*, (McGraw-Hill, 1965).

H. I. Ansoff, 'Managing Discontinuous Strategies Change: The Learning Action Approach', in Ansoff, Bosman and Storm (eds), *Understanding and Managing Strategic Change* (North-Holland, 1982).

R. Cyert, and J. G. March, *A Behavioural Theory of a Firm*, (Prentice-Hall, 1963).

J. W. Fredrickson, and T. R. Mitchell, Strategic Decision Processes: Comprehensiveness and Performance in an Industry with an Unstable Environment, *Academy of Management Journal*, vol. 27, no. 2, 1984, pp. 399–423.

J. R. Galbraith, *Organisational Design*, (Addison Wesley, 1977).

J. H. Grant, and W. R. King, Strategy Formulation: Analytical Normative Models, in Schendel and Hofer (eds) *Strategic Management*, (Little Brown & Co, 1979), pp. 104–22.

C. W. Hofer, and D. E. Schendel, *Strategy Formulation: Analytical Concepts*, (West Publishing, 1978).

G. Hofstede, The Poverty of Management Control Philosophy, *Academy of Management Review*, (July 1978), pp. 450–60.

F. I. Inglefinger, Decisions in Medicine, *New England Journal of Medicine*, vol. 29, 1975, pp. 254–55.

C. E. Lundblom, Still Muddling. Not Yet Through. *Public Administration Review*, vol. 39, 1979, pp. 517–26.

L. B. Lusted, *Introduction to Medical Decision-Making*, (L. C. Thomas, 1968).

A. D. Meyer, Mingling Decision Making Metaphors, *Academy of Management Review*, vol. 9, no. 1, 1984, pp. 6–17.

R. E. Miles, and E. E. Snow, *Organisational Strategy, Structure and Process*, (McGraw-Hill, 1978).

D. J. Miller, M. F. R. D. De Vries, and J. M. Toulouse, Top Executive Locus of Control and its Relationship to Strategy-Making, Structural and Environment. *Academy of Management Journal*, vol. 25, no. 2, 1982, pp. 237–53.

H. Mintzberg, Strategy-Making in three modes. *California Management Review*, vol. 16, no. 2, 1973, pp. 44–53.

H. Mintzberg, Patterns of Strategy Formulation, *California Management Review*, vol. 24, 1978, pp. 934–48.

H. Mintzberg, and J. A. Walters, Tracking Strategy in an Entrepreneurial Firm, *Academy of Management Journal*, vol. 25, no. 3, 1982, pp. 465–99.

C. Perrow, *Organisational Analysis: A Sociological View*, (Wodsworth, 1970).

J. B. Quinn, *Strategies for Change: Logical Incrementalism*, (Richard Irwin, 1980).

W. G. Scott, Decision concepts, in W. G. Scott *Organisation Theory*, 1967, pp. 219–26.

A. A. Thompson, and A. J. Strickland, *Strategy and Policy: Concepts and Cases* (Business Publication Inc. 1978).

A. Wildavsky, *Budgeting as a Political Process*, in D. L. Sills (ed.) The Interventionists' Encyclopedia of the Social Sciences. Cromwell, Collier and MacMillan, 1968, pp. 192–99.

THIRTEEN

The Celtic Woollen Company

ANDREW P. KAKABADSE

Introduction

This case examines *consultancy intervention* and *practice*, highlighting *five* key issues that need to be considered in *positively developing client/consultant relationships*. It is considered that the particular *nature* of the client's *situation* and the personal *ethics* and *values* of the consultant will substantially influence the *outcome* of the intervention.

Theory and background

Consultants occupy third party roles, but it is important to emphasize that not all third parties are consultants. A third party is a person, or group of people, who assists the continued development of an organization by helping to diagnose problem areas, generate new strategies, implement solutions and review the continuous process of change and development (Kakabadse 1986). Third parties are the facilitators who develop activities that are not the responsibility of any full-time employee occupying a line hierarchical position. A third party is the additional member to manager/subordinate or colleague/colleague relationships.

It is misleading, however, to assume that only consultants act as third party facilitators. In an organization, issues of coordination, control, interpersonal relationships, strategy formulation and implementation, influence, positively or adversely, the health and success of the organization. Consequently, it is not uncommon for line managers to assist superiors, peers, subordinates and colleagues in other parts of the organization; in effect be utilized as third party facilitators.

Various approaches to third party intervention are outlined in the literature. Sheane (1978) and Blake and Mouton (1983) advocate that effective third party behaviour involves undertaking a macro/whole systems change approach. However, other writers have adopted a micro-perspective to consultancy practice. Argyris (1970) argues that the true purpose of change interventions is to assist clients in coming to terms with change through free, informed choice. Others similarly adopt such a value-free stance in terms of helping people to work together through third parties by openly examining organizational issues (Beckhard 1969; Schein 1969). Walton (1969) proposes a similar perspective and, in addition, provides an analysis of the processes involved in third party consultation. Finally, Swartz and Lippitt (1975) strongly advocate comprehensive evaluations of the consultation process, in order to pinpoint, for the client and consultant's benefit, the progress made.

Key learning points

Effective consultants are identified as practising *two skills*, the *professional/technical skills* for which the client has contracted the consultant, and *interpersonal* skills which enable the consultant to work and effectively interact with clients. The case focuses on the application of the consultant's interpersonal skills in conducting an intervention. In addition, through examining effective and ineffective behaviour, the case is so structured that the students need to discuss the *personal beliefs* and *values* of the consultant, which in turn can act as a stimulus to a more general debate on the ethics of consultancy practice.

The case centres on the intervention conducted by Neville Sims, the consultant, into the Cetic Woollen Company. Specifically, the case addresses the following *learning points*:

1 Initial problem declaration.
2 Stakeholder analysis.
3 Cultural acclimatization.
4 Ethics of consultancy practice.
5 Intervention continuity.

Initial problem declaration

Two factors need to be considered; the *reasons* given for the *intervention* to the consultant; and the manner of *entry* into the organization. The initial problems presented are, an *inability to manage change*, a need to *examine* the structure of the *organization*, a need to *introduce management training*, and a need to address the problems of particular departments such as personnel, marketing, production and sales. Highlight the fact that Sims offers *little information* and opinion at this initial stage and spends most of his time *asking questions* and *listening*. Sims was attempting to gain his own view of the organization and to *compare different perceptions* of the issues and problems facing the Celtic Woollen Company.

In terms of entry, examine how effectively Sims *negotiated* his *entrance* into the organization. Did he establish *good working relationships* with each of the key directors in order to gain a good foothold into the company? Discuss also the role played by Jim Peters in *facilitating* the introduction of Sims into the organization. The general conclusion to reach is that Sims effectively negotiated his entrance in the company by adopting a *non-threatening posture*, listening to other people's views and needs and thereby gaining their support.

Stakeholder analysis

The case emphasizes the *strategic* nature of consultancy intervention and thereby highlights the *processes* of *strategy formation* and *development*. The process of generating strategies in any organization are considered to contain *quantitative* and *qualitative* elements. The quantitative elements consist of the current financial position of the company, market share, return on investment and the relationship between overhead costs and present profitability. The qualitative elements consist of the *vision* of influential managers, the *status* and bargaining power of certain departments/divisions/units and the *relationship* between managers in the organization. Hence, strategy formation is, in this case, the outcome of negotiations between *stakeholders* in the organization. Stakeholders are persons who have *assumed a strong emotional identity* with a part or parts of the organization or for particular types of work activity and *will work towards* the survival and improvement of their stakeholding. Stakeholders have a great deal to *gain* or *lose* with any changes introduced into the organization and hence their *self interest* acts as a *strong stimulus* for their actions. Explore with the student group the *position* and *opportunities* for the key stakeholders as the two McCardles, Patterson, David Price, Alex Campbell and Jim Peters. Introduce into the discussion the history of the Celtic Woollen Company, and the difficulty that any Company Director, such as Price, Campbell and McIntyre, would face with changes of Chief Executive.

Cultural acclimatization

Culture of organization is an important concept underlying this case. Organization culture refers to the *values, attitudes, norms of behaviour* and *ways of thinking* that are *shared* by different people in the organization. Feelings, behaviours or attitudes that are considered as part of the culture of the organization need to be so *deeply held* by individuals, so as to be described as *'natural'*. An organization may consist of different cultures differentiated by *department, function* or *geographic dispersion*. For further information on organization culture, see the teaching notes for the Industrial Development Authority.

Sims needed to understand the culture of the Celtic Woollen Company in order to appreciate the manner in which individuals lived, worked, made and implemented decisions in the organization. The intervention began with Sims informally meeting key managers in order to identify their perceptions as to the key issues and problems facing the organization. The initial meetings were followed by four workshops and were used as a mechanism for:

- Building relationships so that the consultant *could become credible* and *acceptable* to the managers in the organization.
- Identifying the issues that managers considered *pertinent* to the development of their organization.
- Helping managers to *adjust* to the likelihood of change.

The workshop data was valuable to Sims for two reasons. First, he gathered the necessary information in order to submit a report on the perceived current issues in the organization which could be used as the basis for generating recommendations for future action. Second, he became used to the organization, its values and the behaviour of its managers. It is important to emphasize this second point, as it is considered that effective performance in an organization involves thinking, feeling and behaving in a manner *generally acceptable* to the *majority*. Those who cannot accept the *mores* of their employing organization are likely to face difficulties in terms of their job or career progression. Sims recognized that to operate effectively in a client organization, it was necessary to *project acceptance* of certain important *values* in the organization. Explore with the students the predominant culture of the Celtic Woollen Company. The company is described in the case as a 'split, diversive and somewhat bitchy organization'. Would the students agree with this statement, bearing in mind the family dominated, multinational nature of the company? Time should be spent identifying and analysing those factors that can bring about such a negative orientated culture.

Ethics of consultancy practice

The case highlights the ethical issues in consultancy practice, in particular Sims' involvement in the early retirement of Jim Peters. The questions raise concern as to *who is the client*, and what are the *real issues* underlying the intervention?

'Who is the client?' is a question that needs to be fully debated by the student group. Examine the *sponsorship* of Sims by Peters in gaining *access* to key stakeholders and *organizing* the workshops. Further, Peters was charged with the mission of introducing change into the organization. Under such circumstances, it is understandable that Peters should identify himself as the client. Sims' dilemma is that he unearths data indicating the inadequacy of Peters and the Personnel Department. It could be that Peters recognized the problems in his own department and required a catalyst to stimulate change, a role he hoped Sims would fulfil. However, he did not contract with Sims for change within the Personnel Department. Further, explore the status of Peters as far as the intervention is concerned. Is the 'real' client, Rory McArdle, as his support had to be gained before embarking on particular projects? Sims' difficulties in his relationship with Peters, emphasizes the contentious issues of '*switching clients*' in order to ensure the continuity of the intervention.

A likely response would be to blame Sims as manipulative and unethical. Such a reaction needs to be explored by examining the *underlying* issues in the case. Is the intervention simply a data gathering exercise in order to organize relevant management training programmes, or an intervention of a more strategic nature, looking at future possible courses of action as well as how the organization really functions.

A distinction is drawn between addressing *short term*, as opposed to *longer term*, business problems. Short-term problem solving is equated with *tactics* which are concerned with the implementation of agreed strategies or policies. People need to feel *trust* in one another's abilities to manage situations and feel comfortable when discussing work orientated problems. Working effectively towards agreed goals requires people to be *open* with each other and *share* information in order to generate the *necessary feedback*, in order to be able to adjust performance. Such principles, however, may be difficult to practise in situations where long-term policies and strategies are being generated. Such a process is likely to be fraught with ambiguity. There are likely to exist differences of opinion and a wide range of expressions of intentions for the future as represented by numerous groups or individuals in the organization. The process of strategy development is as much about *developing appropriate strategies* as it is about *vested interests generating policies to suit their needs*.

The attitudes and behaviours required of a consultant in situations of tactical *vs* strategic development are considered to be different. In a tactical consultant interaction, *open, honest behaviour* under the cloak of specialist adviser would be deemed appropriate behaviour. The process of strategy formation and implementation are the result of the negotiations between key stakeholders. Under such circumstances, the consultant is brainstorming and problem solving with key managers as well as *developing* his own views as to the *future direction of the organization*. It would be virtually *impossible* for the consultant *to stand apart* from the process under the cloak of acting as specialist adviser or expert.

Sims discovered that he had to consider the vested interests in the Celtic Woollen Company and finally identify himself with his primary client (Rory McArdle), support him and be prepared to be held accountable for aligning himself with his views concerning the future. Sims could not afford to be identified with the Director of Personnel and hence, allied himself to a 'client' that was safer (McArdle) and strategically powerful in the organization. The ethics of tactical *vs* strategic interventions is outlined in Table 1.

Table 1 *Ethics of consultancy practice*

Tactics *vs* strategy development	
Tactics	*Strategy*
Identify training needs.	Work with senior managers to identify strategies for the future.
Implement training programmes.	Map out the vested interests in the organization.
On the job counselling.	Workshops and conferences for solving long-term problems.
Training through project work.	Identify problems in implementation of strategy.
Brainstorming for new ideas.	Consultant to identify his 'real' client and policies he wishes to pursue.
Workshops for solving short-term problems.	Once strategy is established, tactics can be identified.
Apply a particular specialist package.	

Continuity of intervention

The longer term continuity of the intervention depends partly on the *strength* of *relationships negotiated* by Sims with key stakeholders and partly on the *standards* of *practice* of *professional* consultant skills.

Sims placed executives into key positions in the organization and drafted and implemented the management development blueprint. Sims also seems to have adequately negotiated his relationship with Rory McArdle, but not with other key stakeholders, as Jonathan McArdle. Hence, it is also necessary to examine the *impact of the likely responses of key stakeholders* to the continuity of the interventions.

Explore with the student group how this intervention could continue or should it be brought to a close, in effect, *disengage* from the *client*. Attention needs to be paid to the following questions:

- How should *effective disengagement* take place?
- Is Sims attempting to *gain* further *business* for himself, or attempting to meet the organization's needs under *difficult* circumstances?
- Does the consultant develop sufficiently *strong relationships* to maintain credibility and offer an *adequate service* to the organization (draw attention to the newly appointed executives and how they may feel about Sims).

No particular answer can be given to the above questions other than to highlight the ambiguous nature of strategic type interventions. A great deal depends on who is the *consultant's client(s)*, and how effectively has the consultant '*protected*' his client. What are the *values* and *ethics* of the consultant and how do these *beliefs influence* his *attitudes* in terms of the situations he has had to manage. Further, how competently has he applied, and been perceived to apply, his professional skills. These issues are important even if the intervention is coming to a close. Effective disengagement does *not* mean losing all contact with the organization but having *negotiated an image* of credibility so as to be re-called on an intermittent basis to address particular issues.

Teaching guide summary

Issues	*Learning points*
1 Initial problem declaration.	<ul><li>Declared reasons for intervention.</li><li>Entry process.</li><li>Comparison of different perceptions.</li></ul>

		• Negotiate entry.
		• Negotiating effective client relationships.
2	Stakeholder analysis.	• Vested interests.
		• Strategy formation and development.
		• Quantitative and qualitative elements to strategy formation.
		• Disruptive impact of change on stakeholders.
3	Cultural acclimatization.	• Shared values, attitudes and norms of behaviour.
		• Multiple cultures in organizations.
		• Consultant credibility involves acceptance of the mores of the organization.
		• Key stakeholders could be culture makers.
4	Ethics and consultancy practice.	• Who is the client.
		• Underlying issues of intervention.
		• Switching clients.
		• Tactical *vs* strategic intervention.
5	Continuity of intervention.	• Strength of client/consultant relationships.
		• Personal beliefs of consultant.
		• Professional application of consultant.
		• Effective disengagement.

The teaching guide summary can be prepared for acetate in order to highlight the key learning points at the end of the case discussion.

Teaching style

The class needs to be divided into subgroups in order to address the three questions at the end of the case. Use three white boards or at least three separate sheets of flip-chart paper in order to highlight the contributions of the class in response to each of the three questions respectively. Once all contributions have been received, identify the key learning points, drawing on the evidence of the students' contributions. After further discussion, terminate the session by presenting, on acetate, the teaching guide summary.

References

C. Argyris, *Intervention Theory and Method*, (Addison-Wesley, 1970).

A. Bandura, *Social Learning Theory*, (Prentice Hall, 1977).

R. Beckhard, *Strategies of Organisation Development*, (Addison-Wesley, 1969).

R. R. Blake, and J. S. Mouton, *Consultation: A Handbook for Individual and Organisation Development*, (Addison-Wesley, 1983).

E. Goffman, *Frame Analysis: An Essay on the Organisation of Experience*, Penguin, 1974).

A. P. Kakabadse, 'Consultants and the Consultancy Process,' *Journal of Managerial Psychology*, vol. 1, no. 1, 1986.

J. Mangham, *The Politics of Organisational Change*, (Associated Business Press, 1979.

W. Mischel, 'Self-Control of the Self', in T. Mischel (ed) *The Self: Psychological and Philosophical Issues* (Rundman and Littlefield, 1977).

D. Sheane, 'Organisation Development in Action', *Journal of European and Industrial Training*, vol. 2, no. 8, 1978, pp. 1–31.

J. E. Schein, *Process Consultation: Its Role in Organisation Development*, (Addison-Wesley, 1969).

D. Swartz, and G. Lippitt, 'Evaluating the Consulting Process,' *Journal of European Training*, vol. 4, no. 5, 1975.

R. E. Walton, *Interpersonal Peace Making: Confrontation and Third Party Consultation* (Addison-Wesley, 1969).

FOURTEEN

The Public Welfare Agency

JACQUELINE DRAKE AND ANDREW P. KAKABADSE

Part 2

Which is more important?

'Ok Joan, I hear you. But which is more important, the schedule, the people or the project?' asked Saul.

Joan wondered whether she had made the right choice in hiring Saul Becker. The whole project was now taking too long. Saul had held unstructured interviews, sent round questionnaires and held further one-to-one interviews. In addition, Saul had been holding briefing meetings for various groups, feeding back the initial survey results for the groups to debate and offer suggestions as to the next step. Saul added the briefing groups' suggestions to his data bank. However, he had sensed that Joan was becoming impatient as the study was not progressing at sufficient speed.

'Basically I need to know how people feel so that I can try to improve morale and complete my reorganization,' stated Joan to Saul, at their regularly monthly meeting.

'The information that I am giving you is not sufficient then?' enquired Saul.

'No! I need a complete report so that I can get on with my job of discussing, deciding and implementing the necessary action', responded Joan.

'I must tell you that this survey has generated a lot of interest among the people I have interviewed. They want feedback and I give them feedback. You know, they actually use the information to help them plan their roles and also to work better as teams.'

'Individual groups are very protective of their own activities and geographical areas. There is still a lot of confusion about the boundaries of both since the reorganization. It leads to an overlap of effort. Everyone sees the level above them as interfering rather than managing and those on the same level as competing with them. It has led to a lot of frustration and dissatisfaction and nobody is very skilled at handling it. As a result, everybody does their own thing.'

'The various groups have offered me a lot of good will. I have to respond to that,' said Saul.

'I understand that, but I need some assistance as well, you know,' remarked Joan.

'Look, a common problem with surveys is that it feels as if nothing happens. Some of the people in surveys may feel anxious; others expect action. Either way, the survey has stimulated interest. As surveys and writing reports take time, interest fades. In fact, management may turn out to be in a worse position because people are left with a feeling that nothing happens. In this situation I have responded to some very real needs. People at all levels are using the information to look at themselves and how they operate in their part of the organization. I feel that whatever you want to do from now on, it will make your job easier,' stated Saul.

Pause.

'Joan, I hear you, but what is more important, the schedule, the people or the project?' questioned Saul once more.

'You know that the project and the people are the most important, Saul. What is really at issue is that you went off on your own. All this should have been sorted out with me,' responded Joan gravely.

'For Christ's sake, I just could not predict it was going to take so long,' replied a defiant looking Saul Becker.

Questions

1 What should Saul do now?
2 Why?
3 How?

Part 3

The directors' meeting

'So you think that we are still too centralized then?' asked Joan.

'Looks like it! You've got too many geographic areas and area directors and you need to spend more attention on supervisors and teams,' responded Saul.

'The area directors won't like this – one of their own going out. What's more, Philip Watson – you know, the Assistant Director for field services – could see this as losing part of his empire. He's been one of your supporters. I need him behind me if I'm going to implement what you recommend,' stated Joan.

'What we need to do is present this so that everyone wins. Perhaps I should present the data and then split the directors into two groups with me acting as leader for one and you the other. We can help them identify recommendations which you could use. It will help them have ownership of the data and all further actions,' responded Saul.

'Good idea. Lets work on that,' said Joan.

'It'll probably take a full day,' warned Saul.

Joan invited both the Assistant and Area Directors to the meeting. All attended. The data presentation took one and a half hours. By now Saul was summarizing his findings.

'So to conclude, let me list the key issues identified in this survey.' Saul walked over to the flipchart and began to write:

1   Most social workers, supervisors and some area directors and assistant directors are in favour of the reorganization.
2   Some area directors and assistant directors are not in favour of reorganization.
3   Some area directors are unclear as to their role.
4   Supervisors and social workers want greater emphasis on teams.
5   Supervisors would like training on managing teams.
6   The research function is nonexistent.

Saul had been writing and talking at the same time.

'Any questions?' he asked.

The next two hours were spent on questions and comments.

'It's lunchtime,' said Joan, 'let's resume after lunch. Why not split into two teams to discuss how we could use these findings to make policy recommendations. Saul will lead one team. I will lead the other. Are you in favour?'

Further discussion ensued which led to agreement.

'Ok, let me split the group into two,' offered Saul. He cleverly mixed those who were for reorganization with those who were against; placing Lionel Edgely in Joan's group and Philip Watson in his own group.

It was three and a half hours later when the two groups met in plenary. Joan's group reported first, arriving at the conclusion that further discussion and research was necessary before any practical recommendations could be made. Then Saul's group made their presentation; Philip Watson was the speaker.

'Unlike your group,' pointing to Joan and Lionel, 'we feel we've cracked the problem,' laughed Philip.

He put this group's recommendations on the flip chart:

1 No further research is required in order to make recommendations.
2 All of the group are in favour of the reorganization.
3 The director of social services (Joan) should set aside a budget for the training of supervisors.
4 The organization is still top heavy.
5 One area should be amalgamated into the other areas and one post of Area Director should disappear.
6 The redundant Area Director should be given a research and development responsibility.
7 The director should decide whether research and development merits Assistant Director status.

Philip stopped talking. The plenary went dead quiet for a few seconds.

'Very, very valuable,' stated Joan. 'I really can use these recommendations. Thank you,' she continued.

'Put our group to shame,' stated one of the Area Directors in Joan's group.

'Yeh, we all know why that is,' remarked Tony Blair, pointing a finger at Lionel Edgely.

Apparently, in Joan's group, the Assistant Director, Residential Services, had forced the discussion to concentrate on whether the initial reorganization was valuable, indicating that he was totally opposed to Joan's policies. The group did not even begin to examine the findings of Saul's project.

'Well, we need to sort our disagreements out now,' stated Philip Watson. 'We cannot afford to have any of our senior managers being completely against whatever policies we decide to pursue,' he added.

Further discussion ensued. Joan began to feel that everything that could be achieved, had been achieved. At an appropriate point she intervened: 'Ladies and gentlemen, thank you. We've achieved a great deal today. The Assistant Directors and I will take all the recommendations and discuss them at the next management meeting, which is only five days away. As soon as we've arrived at any conclusions, we'll let you know. Once again, thank you so much. I feel it has been a very positive day and that we're beginning to work as a team. If we do it up here, the others will do it at the lower levels.'

The delegates walked out of the room talking, quite loudly, about the day's events. The general hubble and bubble made Joan feel good. In fact, she tried to remember when she had felt so good.

Question

1   How did Saul handle the meeting?

Part 4

A further reorganization

'So we've agreed then,' summed up Joan. 'We'll take the following steps.'

'First, we'll set up internal training programmes for supervisors. That will be the first responsibility for our new Assistant Director.

'Second, we'll place an internal advertisement for Assistant Director, Organization and Professional Development. 'We've all agreed that if Mary Hollins decided to apply, no one would be opposed to her appointment, that is if she was considered to be the best candidate.

'Third, Phil and I will discuss how to re-shuffle the remaining Area Directors around with the removal of the one area vacated by Mary Hollins' possible move up.

'Fourth, we've drawn up a blueprint as to how we will re-draw area boundaries and which supervisors will go with which Area Director. Phil and I will speak to each of the Area Directors concerning the new areas they will be managing and what will be expected of them.

'Does that summarize everything we've agreed?' finished Joan.

The others responded by nods and murmurs of agreement.

'One last thing. I'd like you, Lionel, to sit with me on the interview board. As you know, in local government, representatives from the treasury, personnel and the chief executive's office also have to sit on an interview board for positions of Assistant Director and above. It's crazy, we're the ones who have to work with this new person in our establishment, but only two of us can represent the department on the interview board,' stated Joan.

Silence.

'Well, are there any other issues?' asked Joan.

'No. Ok. Fine. I think we've achieved a great deal today. Thank you. I am really looking forward to this new challenge. By the next management team meeting, most of these policies will be in operation. Phil, Lionel and I can give our early impressions.'

Joan closed the meeting in her usual optimistic style.

The Assistant Director, Residential Services, thought to himself as he walked out:

'Christ, that woman is smart. She's had everything her own way and she's even got me helping her doing the very thing I don't want to do. Damn her!'

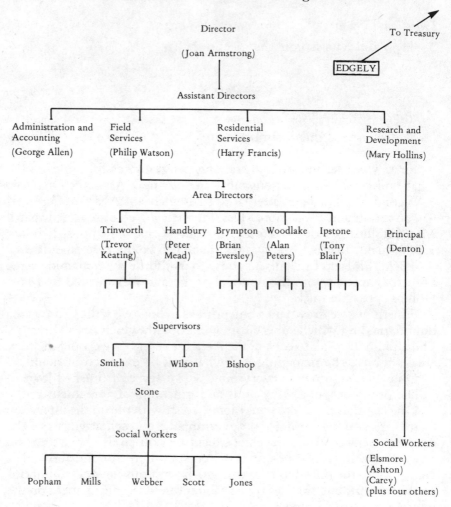

Figure 1   *Social services – organizational structure, post-Saul Becker*

Introduction

This case examines the *dynamics* of *data feedback* as a *mechanism* for *introducing change* into *organizations*. The *three-level data feedback process model* is presented, which identifies *six steps* to introducing and successfully *implementing change* and highlights *three separate levels* of *data feedback*.

Theory and background

Information is the *life-blood* of any organization. Data that has been gathered, organized and presented in particular ways gives people *the knowledge* they need to do their work, to achieve *prescribed standards* and to understand who has the *authority* to direct actions. As information and information exchange are key ingredients in the process of helping organizations operate, then the gathering of new information and its feedback to various personnel in the organization on how effectively people and systems are functioning, is an equally *powerful* tool for adaptation and change (Nadler 1977; 1981).

Consequently, in order to introduce changes into an organization, it is necessary to be aware of *what* data should be gathered from *whom* and *why*! Equally important are process issues, namely *how* is data to be gathered and *how should it be fed back*. Managing the process of data gathering and data feedback really determines whether attempts at change will be a success or failure. Undoubtedly, the quality of the data gathered is a key area of concern but not the final determinant of successful change attempts. Knowing *how to handle* the various parties involved in the change programme is as vital as knowing what quantitative data analysis skills to apply (Kakabadse 1984). *People's feelings* in any data gathering process need to be taken ito account in order to ensure that appropriate data is accurately gathered.

Data feedback is an under-researched area in managerial psychology. Two texts, however, are worthy of attention. Bowers and Franklin's (1977) book on data-based organizational change provides an all-encompassing analysis, examining the nature of organizations, the nature of the processes of change, how to conduct diagnoses and data feedback, the role of the change agent, evaluating interventions and present practices and future needs. Nadler (1977) provides an in-depth analysis, offering case study examples and focusing more than Bowers and Franklin (1977) on the gathering of data, feedback and change within the organization process. Other texts include Bennis' (1966) work emphasizing a rational approach to planned change; the Nadler (1981) treatise on managing macro-change utilizing humanistic values, and Bowers (1973) introduction to data feedback using case study examples.

Key learning points

This four-part case focuses on the intervention of an academic, Saul Becker to conduct a survey of employee opinions and attitudes in a public welfare agency on the invitation of the Director of the Agency. The issues, problems and opportunities confronting Becker need to be fully examined in the discussion of the case. Specifically the case is centred around the six-stage data feedback model.

The stages of data feedback are:

1 Problem sensing.
2 Problem diagnosis.
3 Decision to collect data.
4 Data collection.
5 Data presentation.
6 Strategy implementation.

Throughout the six stages, attention needs to be focused on the *type of data* to gather and the *interpersonal processes* between consultant and client(s).

The manner in which the case discussion takes place is important in order to successfully teach the case. Feedback to the student group is given after discussion of each part of the case. Consequently, analysis of each of the stages is undertaken separately and can be issued as feedback to the students after each part of the case. For further details on how to teach the case, see Teaching Style.

Welfare Agency Part 1 Discussion notes for distribution to students

Stage 1 Problem sensing

Stage 1 involves someone internal or external to the organization *spotting a problem* or a series of related problems. The problems have to be considered sufficiently *important* to require some action before proceeding to Stage 2. Joan Armstrong recognized the poor interpersonal relationships among her Assistant Directors and Area Directors. She was conscious that personal relationships needed to improve in order for her policy of decentralization to work.

Stage 2 Problem diagnosis

Having been deemed worthy of attention, the problems are now defined in terms of whose they are, what impact they have, on whom and at what cost. Who are the '*stakeholders*' (interested parties), how much *power* and *influence* do they have and what have they to *gain* or *lose* by the problems continuing or being solved? What are the apparent causes of the problems and how can the *root cause* be investigated? Encourage the group to identify the stakeholders, such as Tony Blair, Lionel Edgely and Trevor Keating and examine their particular needs and interests.

Stage 3   Decision to Collect Data

This stage signifies the commitment to take action *to find out more* about the problems rather than just speculate on the one hand or jump to hasty solutions on the other. Joan Armstrong recognized that to introduce further change into the organization without any information concerning people's attitudes towards her, her ideas and the organization, would be a costly mistake. She needed additional information to get to the root causes of the problems facing her. Then she would be able to decide on the most appropriate solution and how to win commitment to it. She recognized that she couldn't do this alone. Hence the need for an external consultant.

However, an external consultant *cannot, in isolation, gather appropriate data*. In order for Saul to conduct the project, he needed to win the support of key managers in the organization. His strategy was *client-need orientated*: to identify the needs of various groups in the organization and to gain their support by indicating that the project could help them in meeting certain of their work needs. Gaining the *commitment* of the Assistant Directors and Area Directors was critical. Once they were *convinced the project was valuable*, they would participate, encourage their subordinates to do likewise and accept ownership of the project in terms of wanting to know the results and how to utilize them.

As soon as the decision to collect data is known, *anxieties* can begin to surface. To identify whether people's fears are being raised, it is necessary for the data collectors to be *sensitive* to the *interpersonal processes* involved in data collection. For example, people may seem reluctant to be interviewed or to offer particular documents; people may seem defensive in interviews; it may be difficult to even arrange for an appointment to see people. Such anxieties have to be reduced or else people will ultimately refuse to participate in the study.

To reduce people's fears it is necessary to put in practice smoothing strategies. There exist three *smoothing strategies*:

1   *Prepare groups for data collection*. Identify groups and individuals who may react adversely to a data collection study. Arrange for preliminary meetings with the groups, the individuals and their bosses, explaining why a data collection study is under way, its objectives and possible final outcomes. Encourage individuals at such meetings to talk about their fears so that all potentially threatening issues can be brought out into the open and debated.

2   *Handle each respondent's anxieties during data collection*. It may be necessary whilst interviewing, observing or gathering documentation from individuals to leave aside some time for

openly discussing the data collection study. In this way, the respondents can begin to understand why the study is being conducted and hence have an opportunity to discuss in an informed way, and in comfortable one-to-one surroundings, their reactions to the venture.

3   *Ensure that people's views are taken into account.* As part of the smoothing process, it is necessary to act on the reactions of the respondents. Their views and anxieties should be fed back to all the active members of the data feedback study. In addition, such process data is a good way of testing whether people's perceptions as to the original problems have changed. If people's view of the problems have changed, the diagnosis will probably need to be reconsidered. This in turn will challenge and may modify the decisions regarding the type of data to collect and who should be involved in its collection.

Part 1 discussion notes for Case 1 can be issued to the students at the end of the group discussion.

Welfare Agency Part 2 Discussion notes for distribution to students

Stage 4   Data collection/first level feedback

The data can be gathered in many ways: by questionnaires; by conducting interviews; by holding group meetings or workshops where both the opinions of individuals and groups are taken into account; by observing the behaviour and interactions of particular individuals or groups; by examining specific documents. It can be gathered from random or systematic samples, from entire populations or from selected individuals.

As a consequence of collecting data and involving particular people in the collection process two things happen: the first is that a *need* arises to *feed data back* to certain individuals and groups in the organization. This is described in the data feedback model as Level 1 feedback. The second is that numerous people in the organization will have *recognized* that *new activities* are taking place, such as people being asked questions or questionnaires being distributed for completion. As a response to the data search, people may become fearful that *unexpected* or *unwelcome changes* may be *imminent*. As a defensive measure, certain individuals or groups may reject the data collection process by *refusing* to take part in the exercise. Hence, Level 1 feedback is concerned with identifying and reducing the degree of *shared anxiety* in the system to the collection of data.

Level 1 feedback is aimed at reducing the level of anxiety in the system about the survey and possible future changes in the organization.

Saul was sensitive to his survey participants' needs. He also responded to their interest in the survey. He fed back to them the data relevant to them and took note of their responses. He could see that the process of future change and development would be much smoother if particular groups and individuals were feeling, thinking and discussing change before it was thrust upon them.

However, he had responded to expressed needs in an ad hoc way. His mistake was that he did not attempt to renegotiate his position with his principal client – the Director of the organization. Saul did not fully explore his role with Joan. Joan had indicated that she required a *researcher*. Saul accepted the brief but allowed his role to extend to that of *change agent*; in many ways, a natural development. Either Saul or Joan should have anticipated, or at least observed, this growth in the researcher's role and discussed its implications in terms of the project.

At the same time, *expectations* are raised among the participants in the data gathering sample. This is useful in that it prepares the client system for change but is a *potential source* of *discontent* in that expectations may become unrealistic. It also *diverts* the attention of the consultant from his primary mission and his principal client.

The data collection process itself becomes *interactive* as new findings are easily fed back to client groups for further debate and analysis. This exacerbates the three major problems facing the consultant at this stage:

1 The over-running of time schedules.
2 The frustration of pursuing dead–ends and red herrings.
3 The relentless task of effectively maintaining presence with a continually changing group of second-order clients. The consultant spends a substantial period of time negotiating and maintaining credibility with various personnel in the organization and as a result the key clients are often neglected.

What is required here is an influencing strategy to establish and maintain credibility with various people in the organization and to work out the best way of having an impact at Stage 5 when final data presentation takes place in a formal context.

Part 2 discussion notes can be issued to the students at the end of the group discussion.

Welfare Agency Part 3 Discussion Notes for distribution to students

Stage 5   Data presentation/second level feedback
At Stage 5, the data gathered is presented as findings to the interested parties. Data presentation may involve submitting written reports to

certain individuals or groups; preparing video reports; offering data for discussion in small groups or large group sessions; arranging workshops to discuss the data; organizing training events based on the data; providing exclusive feedback sessions to the key decision-makers in the organization, such as Chairman, Managing Director, members of the board.

The way data is fed back depends on the *impact* that the data collectors wish to make on various members of the organization. The ultimate purpose is to *stimulate* change in the organization. Hence, data feedback at this stage is essentially concerned with *preparing* the various groups and key individuals in the system to think about change. To whom data is offered and the way it is offered are important considerations for the data collectors. The aim is to *influence* the opinion of particular people in the organization in particular ways. Hence, *the collectors need to have established sufficient power influence and credibility to be able to decide*:

- Who is to be fed what information?
- Whether all the respondents are to be fed the same information.
- How the information is to be offered to various groups.
- What the various concerns of different groups in the organization are and to what extent the data should address each group's concerns.
- Whether further working parties should be organised to analyse the value of the data.
- Who should sit on the working parties.
- On the most appropriate way to obtain a general commitment to use the data gathered in a positive way.

People's views of the data and their analysis of the data should be noted by the data collectors for it may alter opinions as to what really are the problems, and whether a second, probably smaller, data feedback survey may result from such discussions.

Particular attention needs to be given to the way Joan attempts to motivate by responding positively to his group's findings, and his comments and recommendations. It is interesting to consider the sort of response and cooperation Joan could expect from Philip Watson in the future.

Level 2 feedback is aimed at influencing key individuals and groups in the organization to think about and generate strategies for change.

The problem that arises out of Stage 5 is that formal data feedback can touch the *core values* of the individuals concerned. What they hold as important to their position and the way they work can easily be threatened by the findings and/or way, in which the findings are presented.

Emerging out of Stage 5 effectively, requires identifying particular solutions to problems.

Part 3 discussion notes can be issued to the students at the end of the group discussion.

Welfare Agency Part 4 Discussion notes for distribution to students

Stage 6   Strategy implementation/third level feedback
This is the final stage of a data feedback survey and is concerned with the *implementation of particular changes.* In order to introduce change that will be supported and recognized as worthwhile in the organization, the smoothing strategies of Stages 3/4 and the manoeuvring and power/politics strategies of Stages 4/5 must have been *effectively applied.*

By introducing changes in the organization, the people who have to implement the changes and accept the changes will also have to adjust their attitude to the way work and relationships are to be conducted. Stage 6 is as much concerned with *influencing* the deeply held attitudes with which most people in the organization identify, as it is with the implementation of change. It is vital that all the personnel involved at the implementation stage should have been prepared to accept change.

The changes could concentrate on improving the *performance* of people, *reorganizing* the range of products or services on offer, *re-examining* task performance and productivity, *reviewing* the technology currently in use and *assessing* whether new technologies would be required in the future, *reviewing* the organizational/divisional and departmental structures currently in operation. In order to achieve improvements in the area of people, products or services, tasks, technology and organization, it is necessary to be *aware of the impact* that change in one area is likely to have on other areas and to take this into account.

As part of the process of examining the practical problems of implementing change, the parties involved should again re-examine how the data feedbck survey began, who collected what data and why, and whether the data collected is still of value at Stage 6. From these questions, further data feedback surveys may result.

Level 3 feedback is aimed at influencing those who are involved with implementation of change, to ensure that the changes are carried out.

Part 4 discussion notes can be issued to the students at the end of the group discussion.

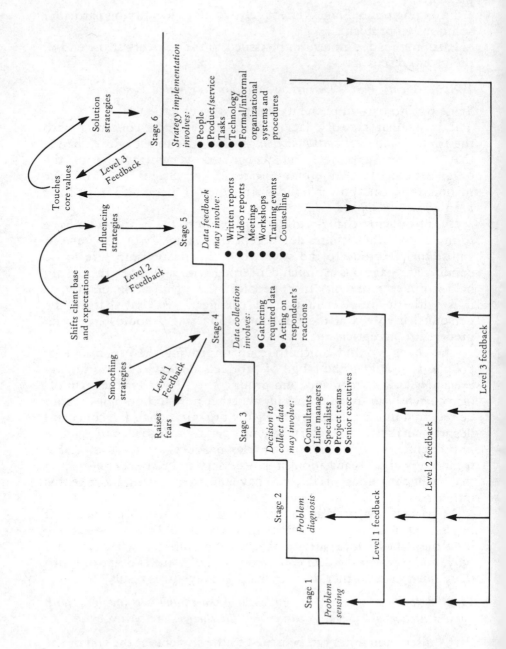

Figure 2: *Data feedback model*

Data feedback model

This is a six-stage model (see Figure 2).

Each stage represents a separate activity. Some of these activities create specific problems which require particular strategies if they are not to jeopardize the overall process. Some stages 'feedback' into one another and may change the basis of earlier decisions. Iterative loops are established and modifications may be made as previous stages are revisited. In effect, the strategies to move on to the next stage, feedback into the problems that gave them life. The skill of the consultant is to move him or herself and his or her clients on, while still handling earlier problems.

Summary

Data feedback is a highly effective means of influencing people's *values*, *attitudes* and *norms of behaviour* in order to introduce, or prevent, change. In applying data feedback approaches, it is important to realize that *the data* and the *process of data collection* are equally important in the change intervention. The data gathered provides the fuel for the debate on what should be done, how and by when. The process of data collection provides the data collectors with information about people's feelings concerning their work, their superiors, subordinates and colleagues, their strength of identity with the status quo and their reactions to change. Both *quantitative* and *qualitative* data have to be taken into account in any data feedback survey.

Teaching guide summary

Issues	Learning points
1 Problem sensing.	• Spotting a problem.
	• Approaches to problem exploration.
2 Problem diagnosis.	• Who are the stakeholders.
	• Stakeholder power and influence.
	• Identify root cause of problem.
3 Decision to collect data.	• Meet client organizations' need.
	• Sensitive to client anxieties.
	• Apply smoothing strategies: Prepare groups for data collection

	Address respondents Anxieties during data collection Ensure respondent views are taken into account.
4 Data collection/first level feedback.	• Various techniques of data feedback. • Client curiosity for data feedback. • Reduce degree of shared anxiety. • Need to clarify researcher/change agent role. • Raising client expectations. • Interactive nature of data feedback.
5 Data feedback/second level feedback.	• Data feedback to stakeholders. • Key consideration is the way data is fed back. • Impact of data in order to stimulate change in organization. • Data collectors must decide on manner of data feedback. • Data feedback can be perceived as a threatening process.
6 Strategy implementation/third level feedback.	• Implementing change. • Also influencing deeply held shared attitudes. • Change would affect some or all parts of the business.

Teaching style

This is a sequential case and has to be taught as such. The participants should consider Part 1 in subgroups, and address themselves to the four questions at the end of Part 1. Regroup the participants in the plenary and request views, ideas and evidence in response to the four questions. Take down the key points offered on flipcharts. Issue Part 1 feedback on completion of class discussion. After the participants have read the feedback ask for immediate comments, taking down any views and statements offered on flipcharts. Issue Part 2 of the case for the group to consider in their subgroups. Blutack the group's responses to Part 1 on to a classroom wall. Repeat the process until all four parts of the case and appropriate feedback has been issued.

In the final summary of the case, draw to the group's attention their views, as recorded on flipchart, highlighting the learning points in each part of the case. Emphasize the issues and potential pit falls of the process of data feedback. Draw attention to the blurring of roles between researcher and consultant.

Conclude the session by presenting on acetate the teaching guide summary and Figure 1 – the data feedback model – indicating that 'smoothing' the anxieties of respondents is as important as gathering and feeding back appropriate data.

References

W. G. Bennis, *Changing Organisations* (McGraw-Hill, 1966).

D. G. Bowers, 'OD Techniques and their Results in Twenty-three Organisations: The Michigan ICL Study,' *Journal of Applied Behavioural Science*, vol. 9, 1973, pp. 21–43.

D. G. Bowers, and J. L. Franklin, *Data-Based Organisational Change*, (University Associates Inc. 1977).

A. P. Kakabadse, Training for Change: The Value of Data Feedback, in Kakabadse and Mukhi *The Future of Management Education*, (Gower, 1984).

D. A. Nadler, *Feedback and Organisation Development: Using Data-Based Methods*, (Addison-Wesley, 1977).

D. A. Nadler, 'Managing Organisational Change: An Integrating Perspective.' *Journal Applied Behavioural Science*, vol. 17, 1981, pp. 191–211.

FIFTEEN

Fosbar Electronics

RON LUDLOW

Introduction

The case of Fosbar Electronics examines the problems of management and career development in an organization. It examines the management of choice in undertaking management and supervisory responsibilities, and the interaction between communication and internal motivation.

Theory and background

Most boards of directors would want one of the main objectives of management development to be that of attempting to obtain improved results through improved performance, while helping managers to realize their maximum potential. One major purpose is certainly that of helping the organization to adapt to technological and socio-economic change, while providing appropriate career progressions for all managers, in the context of balancing the short- and long-term needs of both the individual and the organization. The key issues are therefore:

1 Improvement of organizational performance.
2 Developing competent managers.
3 Considering external trends and pressures in the environment.
4 Balancing short and long term needs of the organization.
5 Considering the needs for managers' career and personal development.

Matching achievement of organizational objectives and the satisfaction of individual needs is achieved by careful recruitment, selection and development. Communication is the link which enables organizations and individuals to perceive the amount of match there exists and to generate internal motivation within the individual.

Key learning points

The case concentrates on the choice made by Reg Fryer, the Head of a Department in filling a post which has been left vacant by promotion of its incumbent. In particular the following points, during case discussion, are worth drawing to the students' attention:

1 The management of choice.
2 Supervisory responsibilities.
3 Management and career development.
4 Communication.
5 Internal motivation.

The management of choice

In Fosbar Electronics, Reg Fryer, the Head of the Electronics Department, had to fill a vacancy caused by the promotion of one of his group leaders, Jack Savage, to project leader for a major project. He does seek the opinion of Jack Savage (the outgoing group leader) as to 'the right man for the job', but Jack is unwilling to comment. It must be Reg's decision, because Reg will have to work with whoever is chosen. The two possible candidates were Jack's subordinates, and as such Jack had more immediate and deeper knowledge of them and their capabilities than Reg, who was a further rung up the hierarchy. Jack, in fact, abdicates responsibility for making any recommendation as to his possible successor to Reg Fryer.

Reg Fryer appoints *Gareth Stevens*, a man who has:

- Superior academic qualifications.
- Broad software knowledge/narrow skill knowledge.
- Worked on applications for capital equipment.

YET

- Has little sense of humour.
- Whose work lacks clarity of presentation.
- Has refused to train new graduates.
- Has previously refused supervisory responsibility within his own section, until it was forced upon him.
- Has little contact with other disciplines in the course of his normal work.

147

He does not appoint *Len Bartholomew*, a man who:
- Has been at the firm longer.
- Has broader work experience, has 'risen through the ranks' – workshops, drawing office, etc.
- Has a wide variety of skills.
- Has a reputation for being able to 'think on his feet'.
- Has good negotiating skills and patience.
- Has had responsibility for training new graduates.
- Is a section leader in a department which has close links with production and marketing.

YET

- Has inferior academic qualifications.
- Has little software knowledge.
- Has no aptitude for detailed work.
- Has an irreverent sense of humour which disturbs Reg Fryer.

Reg Fryer made a subjective judgement, weighed up what appeared to him to be the important strengths and weaknesses of both Len Bartholomew and Gareth Stevens, and, not without some unspoken doubts, selected Gareth Stevens to be the new Group Leader. He did not consult with either man during the course of his decision-making. The promotion was announced formally by the posting of a new organizational chart on Reg Fryer's secretary's wall. There was no informal communication by Reg to Len with respect to the reasons why he had not been selected for the new position.

It is interesting to consider some of the reasons why Reg Fryer chose Gareth Stevens rather than Len Bartholomew. These are closely related to the congruence of Reg Fryer's and Gareth Steven's management styles, and the non-congruence of those of Reg Fryer and Jack Savage, the outgoing group leader. Fryer's style could be described as 'remote' (this is supported by the methods he uses to communicate within his department). Jack Savage's style is more person-centred. He leaves Len Bartholomew alone to get on with it. He trusts Len to shout for help if he needs it. All he requires are progress reports which are short and succinct: he appreciates that Len Bartholomew is at a high stage of development with respect to the tasks he is required to perform, and is very willing to delegate accountability and autonomy for those tasks to Len. However, Gareth Steven's style is very production-centred and task-orientated. Unlike Jack, Gareth wants to know details of every task upon which Len is engaged. This can be related to Gareth's background in analysis and reporting.

Supervisory responsibilities

Gareth Stevens has always avoided supervisory responsibilities, both for his own section and the new graduates.

When he is given supervision of Len, he starts off by trying to supervise him closely, wanting to know the exact details of his work in progress. This annoys Len, who has been used to the more relaxed and delegative style of Jack Savage. The wisdom of this approach can be questioned given Len's background and task-specific ability, skills and motivation.

However, when Len's annual review is due, Gareth defers to Len's wishes and allows him to fill in his own assessment. This could either be regarded as a conciliatory gesture towards Len, whom he had previously annoyed by his close scrutiny of Len's work schedule, or as avoiding supervisory responsibility (part of that responsibility being to assess the performance of subordinates).

Management and career development

Both Len and Gareth are section leaders at the beginning of this case. Yet, Len complains of the lack of management training at Fosbar Electronics. His desire for in-company re-training is blocked by his Head of Department because there are inadequate funds available.

Gareth's technical background is narrow. He has twice avoided supervisory responsibilities. Yet, no mention is ever made of the company intending to provide management training for Gareth, although he has now been promoted to the position of Group Leader.

Len needs training in technical skills to advance his career. Gareth needs management development training to improve his interpersonal skills and increase his awareness/knowledge of his management role. Yet, in neither case have these needs been addressed or even identified by the company.

Communication

Reg Fryer has very poor interpersonal skills. At no time does he interview either Gareth or Len, prior to making his decision on the new appointment. After he has decided whom to appoint, he does not communicate his decision verbally, but merely posts a new edition of the 'family tree' on his secretary's office wall.

Therefore the first occasion that Len knows of the appointment is when a technician draws his attention to this revision. He is naturally very angry.

Poor communication has resulted in engendering a feeling of anger and loss of status in Len. He confronts Reg, expressing resentment at being 'leap-frogged.' Reg is then forced to have an explanatory talk with Len. He should have had it before making public the news of the appointment.

Gareth Stevens also has poor communication skills. His need to know the details of Len's work cannot be refuted, but his way of handling the matter shows insensitivity towards a person who was previously his peer. He should have been more tactful in his dealings with Len, appealed to him for help – made Len understand his 'need to know'. The way he handled the matter resulted in Len interpreting his interest as being 'intrusive and insulting.'

Internal motivation

Len Bartholomew was a relatively low-achiever at school. However, his subsequent educational and career development shows a fair degree of self-motivation. This is not impeded by his initial disappointment over Gareth's promotion. He concerns himself with trying to improve an area of personal technical weakness.

When this is blocked through financial strictures within the company, he concentrates on trying to produce a set of modules for use on data transmissions. This is an area where he has a fair degree of expertise. However, he is again blocked by inadequate funds for development.

He can neither improve his technical knowledge nor fully utilize his expertise. Personal development is impossible. In the following months, even the routine work seems to be drying up. This poses a threat to his useful occupation. Len realizes that in the current situation, job fulfilment and promotion are unlikely at Fosbar Electronics. Moreover, he is forty-eight years old.

Len is experiencing a crisis of career and a crisis of confidence.

Teaching guide summary

Issues	*Learning points*
1 Communication.	• The communication process.
	• Formal and informal communication in organizations.

	• Styles of communicating:
	    upwards
	    sideways
	    downwards.

	• Information sharing.
	• Consultation and involvement in decision-making.

- Organizational and personal constraints to effect of communication.
- Executive judgement.
- Announcement and dessemination of decisions which had been made.

2 Managing.

- Making decisions for subordinates rather than with them.
- Identification of both managers' and subordinates' personal goals.
- Short-term and long-term decision-making.
- Perceptual biases (e.g. congruence or noncongruence of management styles).
- Managerial values.
- Living with decisions.

3 Management and career development.

- Identification of organizational and personal needs.
- Shared and unshared meaning.
- The demotivating effect of unrealized expectations.
- Criteria for promotion particularly for professionals in organizations.

  e.g. is seniority, either departmental or company-wide, an important factor to consider?

- Identifying potential.
- Assessing people.
- Performance appraisal and review – the link with management development.
- Motivating managers whose career progression has been blocked.

4 Internal motivation.	• Causes of internal motivation. e.g. intrinsic and extrinsic rewards, satisfaction of personal needs.
	• The varying personal needs of managers at different stages in their careers.
	• Job design.
	• The effect of organizational climate on internal motivation.
	• Boss/subordinate relationships.
	• Delegation and supervisory responsibilities.
	• Involvement in decision-making.

Teaching style

Make available three white boards/black boards.

Ask the groups to present the results of their discussion of each question. Write on the white boards/black boards the key findings of each group. After the groups have finished their presentations fit their findings into the structure of the teaching guide on a separate board. As the key points emerge and are identified by the groups, explore and discuss with the class whether they recognize these key points in the case and relate these key points to their own work/job environment.

In the closing summary of the case, highlight the importance of organizations effectively structuring management development processes within their organizations; and the urgent need for these processes to be thoroughly communicated and understood by managers within their organizations, and that unrealized expectations can become demotivators.

SIXTEEN

Olde England Taverns

TIM NORMAN AND
JACQUELINE DRAKE

Introduction

Originally written as a business policy case, Olde England Taverns is a good end of term case which *sets organizational behaviour (OB) issues into a broader context*. Part 1 provides a comprehensive review of the brewing industry and Part 2 the workings of a typical company within that industry. It draws attention to the *interrelationship between an organization's culture, structure and strategies*. The inclusion of financial and economic data give additional creditability to OB as a subject and vital information from which to interpret behaviour – particularly *the development of a culture*. The culture that emerges in OB provides a provocative illustration of 'cheating' by individuals and of *the impact of frequent reorganizations*.

This case is also appropriate to a general programme such as 'management of the service industries'.

Theory and background

The case is sufficiently comprehensive to act as an illustrative vehicle for a number of theoretical models/viewpoints. Those mentioned in these notes are Handy's classification of cultures (1978); Mars' classification of fiddles (1983) and Schein's career anchors (1978). Other possibilities are as wide ranging as Peters and Waterman's criteria for excellence (1982) to Kakabadse's organizational politicians (1983).

Scheduled at the end of a programme, this case allows for the application of much that has already been taught.

Part 1 The brewing industry

What's happening in the industry?

The major brewers have become increasingly competitive with one another. Once conservative and defensive towards change, they have been forced, by technical developments in production and distribution, to take a more aggressive competitive stance. In addition, national brands and concentration of ownership have made the industry attractive to non-brewers.

The most crucial market trend to affect the brewers has been the static demand for beer in the past decade and fall in demand during the last three years. In public houses (PHs) the most important trends have been the increasing consumer interest in lager, wines, food and entertainment and increasing competition from other retail outlets such as clubs and supermarkets.

What strategies have been adopted to meet these changes, and why?

The three major markets in which the brewers now compete are the PHs, the retail chains and the free trade. They have adopted a different competitive strategy in each:

- In their PHs they compete on the amenities and services offered.
- To supermarket and off-licence chains they compete on price, especially for lagers and wine.
- Within the free-trade they compete by offering low or nil interest loans to publicans and club owners in order to persuade them to purchase their products.

The reasons why these strategies have been adopted are:

1   That in order to maintain volume, the brewers have had to use the supermarkets to sell their products. The cost to the brewers of utilizing the massive retailing capabilities of them however has been lower margins. The buying power of the retail chains has forced the brewers to sell their products at lower prices than they charge their own i.e. lower than internal transfer prices.

The pressure on the brewers to maintain volume is because modern brewing plant is both large in capacity, and also expensive to operate and maintain. The concentration of the brewing firms has made them vulnerable to falls in beer demand, because the sheer size of the breweries means that a plant closure results in a significant fall in the productive capacity of a brewing firm. Consequently, the brewers have to keep volume up to cover the high fixed costs, and can only close a plant when there has been a large decline in beer demand.

The brewers have therefore had to trade-off the costs of keeping their breweries open against the loss of profit margin, because they sell cheaply to the retail chains.

2   That the free-trade also offers the brewers the opportunity to keep sales volumes up, although without having to sell their products as cheaply as they have been obliged to do when selling to the retail chains.

3   That in order to recoup some of the losses on margins, the brewers have actively followed a policy of high pricing in their own PHs. To justify this policy they have invested heavily in their PHs, by improving the decor, catering facilities and toilets etc. The investments made by the brewers have also been undertaken to expand their retail operations away from the common pub and into restaurants, fast-food outlets, cocktail bars, theme pubs and night-clubs.

Part 2 Olde England Taverns (OET)

What are the key issues associated with the management of decentralised profit centres in International Leisure (IL)?

Issue 1   Success of OET's strategies (business policy/finance).
Issue 2   Success of OET's expansion into non-pub operations (management style).
Issue 3   Success of decentralisation in I.L. (culture/structure).

Issue 1 How successful were OET's strategies?
Have the brewers, through the example of OET, been successful in their strategy of improving their PHs and at the same time, of keeping prices high? Have they been able to maintain their overall PH profitability? Or, has the strategy resulted in a fall in profits? Finally, what rate of return has been earned from the investments that have been made?

OET and the investment spree
Between the years 1977 and 1982 OET invested nearly £100m in its estate. During this period the gross margin on the company's sales rose from 40.8 to 45.9 per cent. Clearly OET was allowed by its holding company FEHB, to follow the strategy of high selling prices and improving amenities in its PHs.

But the company's profits did not increase sufficiently to justify the amount of invest~   :t was allowed to make. In 1977 the average n~+   in OET was £8,794, and by 1982 this
'   However, if the contribution from

Machine Income (MI) is taken out of these calculations, the average house net profits were £5,837 in 1977 and only £3,797 in 1982. In other words, the profitability of each OET PH fell on average by 35 per cent during the five year period.

Given this scenario of falling unit profitability, it can be concluded that the rate of return from its investments was at best a nil return, and that most of the £100m was wasted. Approximately, £65m was invested in order to achieve a commercial rate of return, while the rest (£35m) was used to maintain the estate. It is the £65m which was used to improve amentities and from which the company's growth was to come.

Therefore, although OET consistently raised prices it is clear that its customers were not willing to pay those prices, even in return for better surroundings and facilities offered by the OET PHs. The company increased its margins, but had to suffer lower profitability.

The effect of MI on OET's profits is crucial, in that its contribution to net profit increased from 34 per cent in 1977 to 73 per cent in 1982. This very rapid growth in MI could not have been foreseen by the brewers or OET. As such it cannot form part of the strategy which was undertaken, and can therefore be legitimately taken out of the calculations of unit profitability.

Issue 2 How successful was OET's expansion into non-PH operations? The Merlin and Pickwick experiments were both financial failures. However, the company's decision to continue them indicated the seriousness with which the industry was diversifying away from its traditional business. As the fast food market was booming at this time, ventures such as Merlin and Pickwick were not expected to fail. Investment funds and managerial freedom were both available; the key variable remaining was the quality of the managers.

The OET experience illustrates the incompatibility of three different styles of management:

- The OET ex-service, macho, 'clubby' approach, traditional in the brewing industry.
- The tight control and lack of individual discretion characteristic of the fast food industry.
- The individualistic entrepreneurial freedom typical of International Leisure.

Each style is part of a completely different culture and it was the inevitable clash of these cultures that caused OET to fail in its expansionist policy.

Management style in OET
The changes of the 1950s and 1960s (the growth of lager, national brands and the increasing competition in the free-trade) were only taken on board reluctantly.

External factors, such as the influence of United Breweries, and the potential take-overs from non-brewing firms, interested in asset-stripping, forced the brewers into defensive mergers.

The mergers were usually made between firms who were managed by men who knew each other, and who were often friends. The 'clubby' culture was sufficiently strong to prevent United Breweries from gaining a stronghold in the market.

The emphasis on man-management in the industry, and the 'clubby' culture encouraged ex-service personnel to join the industry and in fact to become the dominant group in the brewers' management. OET was no exception to this feature.

Within OET a 'macho-style' of management developed, with many of the senior managers and of the board having ex-service backgrounds. There was therefore a tendency for those with similar backgrounds to be hired, and promotion was obviously more likely for those who either had, or copied, the company's cultural style.

The development of the OET culture was by no means without reason. The loss of takings due to PH managers' fraud necessitated strong, powerful personalities in the line management. The training given in the services is generally believed to breed this kind of manager. But, is this background adequate when the demands of the industry also includes the control and management of investment projects? Clearly the lack of any return on capital invested in OET and the 13 per cent overspend on the large projects would indicate that it is insufficient.

Management style in the fast food industry
All the important managerial decisions in the fast food industry are made centrally leaving little discretion to operating staff. Demands of the fast food industry include:

- Tight stock control.
- Standard costing of products.
- Consistency of quality and product control.
- Employing young staff, often of West Indian or Chinese extraction.
- Managing a split-shift system.
- Utilization of sophisticated catering equipment.
- Using computerised point of sales till.

None of these demands are faced by the average brewery firm line-manager, and there is nowhere, other than the fast food industry itself, from which a manager can gain the necessary experience. OET employed Directors and General Managers who had had necessary experience in the catering industry and who conformed to the OET cultural style. That was sufficient for the OET board to invest £7m and accumulate losses of nearly £2m in the two catering operations which it undertook.

Not all the experiments attempted by the brewers have failed, as the Pizza Hut operation started by Whitbread illustrates. This has been a success, but is probably due to the involvement of the franchisor, the Pepsio Corp. The lack of involvement of the Merlin franchisor, Tasty Burgers, and the limited training of senior management in OET merely added to the problem caused by the criteria for selecting managers.

Management style and International Leisure
The culture in IL totally reflected the management style of its founder, Frederick Goldstein, who was ruthlessly entrepreneurial right up until his death in 1983. His business deals were increasingly 'spectacular' and the big takeovers 'strongly contested' and 'bitterly fought'. He was, in Handy's terms, a Zeus running a power culture. The mastermind behind IL's expansion, Goldstein had little interest in the day-to-day running of the business. Consequently, the decentralized style of management in International Leisure suited him and his HO which was staffed mainly by finance specialists. Their interest in the International Leisure subsidiaries was restricted to whether they were cash-generators or cash-users. OET was a cash-generating business, with £234m sales in 1982. This helped lubricate other parts of the International Leisure empire. In return, OET could reinvest any trading surpluses back into its PHs or other entrepreneurial opportunities e.g. Merlin.

The managerial freedom given to the OET board coincided with the International Leisure style and with the changing needs of the industry towards catering and non-beer products. OET was set up to manage this change in the industry. The argument for its establishment emphasized the need for it to be a separate, independent part of FEHB.

So, despite the outcome of falling profits, wasted investment and failure to perform in the new food market, OET was allowed to continue with little interference from above. Nevertheless, the occasional thunderbolt may strike, as Tom Oliver was well aware, and there was a tradition of change in IL. These too were Goldstein inspired. For example, the removal of all East Ham senior management on take-over. It was part of the culture – there were 'substantial changes in other parts of the Division that hadn't performed'.

Issue 3 How successful was the decentralized style of IL in OET? Of the many possible criteria for success, those of greatest importance to IL were that OET generate cash and that it achieve a 20 per cent return on capital invested. Managerial success within OET would emphasize an efficient administration, a well-motivated workforce and the effective deployment of personnel. All three were critically affected by the *organizational structure* of OET which, in turn, was influenced by the *organizational culture.*

The OET culture
Goldstein's management style established a culture which permeated down right through his empire. The hire and fire/buy and sell attitude, typical of a power-orientated entrepreneur, was converted into numerous reorganization by the more role-orientated managers running OET. These ex-officers, still influenced by their previous paternalistic culture, sought solutions within the company using existing personnel. They had not been trained to 'fire' people. In Schein's terms they probably had quite strong security anchors (having twice attached themselves to large, safe, organizations) and would expect their subordinates to share similar values to themselves. The power culture in which they now found themselves fed their macho self-image but led to somewhat 'cavalier' behaviour rather than tough decision-making. They were not shrewd as businessmen as shown by the Merlin and Pickwick projects nor were they 'hard' as man-managers as evidenced by their unwillingness to confront poor performers.

It was not until one reached the interface with the public that the entrepreneur reappeared – as the pub manager. Like Goldstein, he wanted the freedom to buy and sell, to hire and fire, and to see the cash coming in. Unfortunately this frequently expressed itself in fraudulent behaviour, which also became part of the culture. The 'hidden economy' in Mars' typology.

The rewards and threats dispensed by Zeusian characters, like Goldstein, influence the culture in the form of 'perks' as lesser individuals display their power. Elaborate systems are devised to decide who is eligible for what, how frequently and for what reason. An informal system also emerges to abuse and enhance the formal system. This too becomes part of the culture. The high level of autonomy in OET provided the opportunity for a creative interpretation of 'rewards' together with the threat of their withdrawal. Mars' classification on his grid/group matrix provides a useful framework for categorizing the different groups of people in OET, IL and the fast-food industry. Discussion can then be focused on what constitutes a 'fiddle' and, given the nature of the work in OET, how much latitude should be given to (and by) pub managers. The control and motivation of staff at all levels in OET hinged on a delicate balance of reciprocity to 'get the show on the road' each night. Double standards proliferated. If caught, offenders were not prosecuted; if sacked, they might be re-employed yet they were not paid a 'proper' salary. Under performers were not fired, they were moved sideways in reorganizations.

OET structure
The structure set up in 1976 is shown in Figure 1. Reorganizations in 1978 and 1980 are shown in Figures 2 and 3 respectively.

Reorganizations were seen as solutions to existing problems rather than meeting the challenge of the future. They were a covert form of internal recruitment and de-selection at *all* levels. Organization structures frequently reflect political manoeuvring rather than a response to administrative or market needs.

Implications of the reorganizations
One result of the establishment, and subsequent reorganization, of OET was a 260 per cent increase in administrative costs between 1977 and 1982. This was due to:

- The proliferation of operating companies and regional offices, each with a full managerial team.

- The transfer of PHs from one company to another.

- The fact that many of the operating companies were also 'limited', thus attracting additional administrative costs associated with the production of statutory accounts etc. By 1982 there were sixteen operating companies in OET.

OET was set up therefore in the knowledge that any potential economies of scale which could be gained by keeping OET's administration within FEHB would be forsaken. The argument for having self-contained operating companies in OET was that it passed on the managerial freedom given to OET by IL.

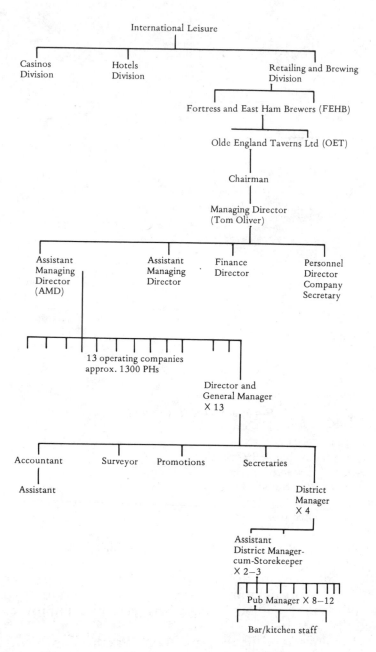

Figure 1 *OET structure (1976)*

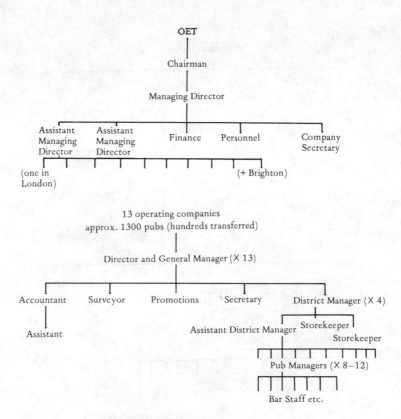

Figure 2 *OET structure (1978)*

Summary of changes
One company disbanded (London)
One company created (Brighton)
Hundreds of PHs transferred from one company to another
Assistant District Manager-cum-Storekeeper Roles split
Some new Directors and General Managers and District Managers internally recruited, older ones retired
Some pub managers transferred to larger or smaller PHs.

It was this freedom that allowed OET to reorganize every other year. These reorganizations plunged OET into an almost constant state of change, without gaining any perceived improvement in profits.

A second result of the reorganizations was that they hindered the assessment of individual managerial performance. The PH transfers

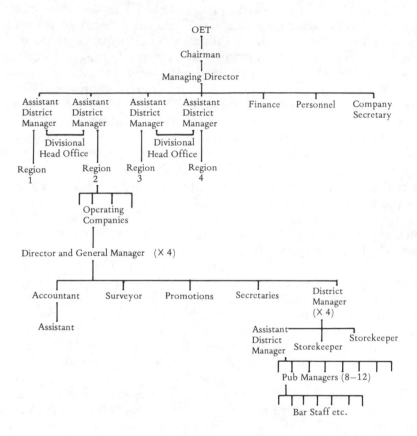

Figure 3 *OET structure (1980)*

Summary of Changes
+300 Fortress PHs
+50 Albany PHs   approx 1600 PHs
+2 Assistant District Managers = 4 Assistant District Managers
+4 Regions = one per Assistant District Manager
   (4 Companies per Assistant District Manager = 16 operating Companies)
+2 Div HOs
Reallocation of PHs to Companies
Some new Directors and General Managers and District Managers internally recruited, older ones retired
Some pub managers transferred to larger or smaller PHs.

meant that there was no continuity of management for the PHs involved in the reorganizations. The transfer of the profits plans of the PHs as part of the reorganizations resulted in the plans being disowned by the Director and General Manager receiving them. It was therefore difficult to assess the trading performance of the PHs transferred because the Director and General Manager receiving them often argued that the plans were unrealistic. This was especially true for those PHs which had been redecorated or restyled for a different clientele. The Director and General Manager receiving them would often argue that the redecoration had been done badly and/or had been overspent against budget, or that the restyling was inappropriate. Consequently there was frequently no one who would accept responsibility for investment failures. The ultimate result of the reorganizations was that it was impossible for the PHs concerned to have a continuity of management. It was difficult to assess the year-on-trading performance of the PHs transferred and to assess the line managers' ability to operate those PHs. Finally, it was difficult to assess the line managers' ability to manage capital projects.

One of the objectives of the reorganization in 1978 was to shorten the lines of communication but, in fact, the change in role for the Assistant District Managers effectively established another managerial level. This was because the reorganization separated the Assistant District Manager-cum-stocktaker job into two individual positions placing the status of the Assistant District Manager between the District Manager and the stocktaker, another managerial layer was created.

The reorganizations therefore had a detrimental effect on OET. They made it difficult to hold the line managers accountable for the performance of their districts. This was an extension of the lack of accountability which OET had to International Leisure. This was because of the decentralized style of International Leisure.

Were the OET reorganizations beneficial in meeting the demands of the changing market? Were there any forces outside OET which hindered their achieving these demands?

- OET was unable to manage the investment funds given to it by International Leisure.
- OET was unable to recruit the right managers for special projects like Merlin and Pickwick.
- OET did not recruit line managers who were able to manage capital projects and create new businesses because the overwhelming requirement placed on the line managers by OET was that

they were to be man-managers. The operational demands of negotiating with PH managers resulted in a management team unsuited to deal with investment and new projects.

- OET did not sack mediocre line managers, and so the reorganizations did not result in a 'shake-out' of bad line managers. All the reorganizations did was to 'shuffle' the pack.

- Finally, OET failed because it was unwilling to alter its management culture which encouraged the recruitment of 'man-managers' rather than retail specialists, which it needed, if it was to take advantage of the changing market.

External reasons for OET's failure to profitably meet the demands of the changing market included FEHB's pricing policy. By offering lower prices to retail chains, FEHB was effectively putting OET's managed houses and FEHB's tenanted houses at a disadvantage. The process of competing against itself was continued by offering loans to free houses in order for them to sell FEHB products. The free trade spent the money on improving their amenities and facilities, in direct competition with the brewer's managed houses. The very advantage which OET sought to gain by PH improvement was compromised by their own holding company. At the same time, the free houses were able to offer the brewer's products at far lower prices than the brewer's own PHs were charging.

In addition, through their strategy with the retail chains, the brewers actively stimulated the market for cheap take-home products. They also promoted the growth of the free trade, particularly that of the licensed restaurateur. This was one of the market sectors in which OET was set up to be successful.

The strategies of FEHB to maintain their volumes conflicted with those of OET. This may not have been the case if International Leisure had had a clear corporate plan and had managed its divisions with greater central control. Instead it allowed OET and FEHB to actively compete against each other. One of the results of this was to undermine the OET investment policy, therefore contributing to OET's failure to obtain a commercial return from its investments.

Summary (bringing Parts 1 and 2 together)

In response to the changing market the brewers adopted three strategies. The OET case demonstrates that the strategies were in conflict with each other when applied in International Leisure. The conflict was allowed to continue because of the decentralized management style within International Leisure. In the case of OET, the problems brought about by the conflict of strategies was exacerbated, because the company's management was unable to handle the demands placed on them. These included the managing of large capital projects and of new businesses in which OET's management had little experience.

As far as International Leisure was concerned, they got the cash they wanted without much difficulty. In addition, the oligopolistic power of the brewing industry and the geographic concentration of PHs meant that the brewers (including FEHB) controlled the supply of beer, wines and spirits to all their managed houses at profitable terms.

Part 2 Olde England Taverns

What are the skills required to function effectively in decentralized profit centres in IL?

1 Political skills
   • keeping IL happy with cash
   • influencing FEHB not to undermine OET's efforts
2 Management skills
   • control systems
   • self-awareness of own strengths and weaknesses
3 Interpersonal skills:
   • assertive communication – ongoing performance
                               – fraud
   • interviewing skills   – selection
                               – appraisal
                               – counselling

Teaching guide summary

Issues	Learning points
1 Brewing industry.	• Impact of changing technology.
	• Major trends affecting brewers/PHs.
	• Different markets need different strategies.
2 Strategy in OET.	• Profitability: apparent *vs* actual.
	• Investment policy: 'stick to the knitting'.

3	Management style.	• Culture dependent. • Problems of inappropriate style.
4	Organization culture.	• Influence of founder. • Decentralization: uses and abuses of autonomy.
5	Organization structure.	• Initial choice. • Reasons for reorganization. • Implications for reorganization.

6	Failure and success by OET.	• Failure
		   internal/external reasons
		• Success
		   IL gets its cash
		   oligopolistic industry.

7	Skills.	• Political. • Management. • Interpersonal.

Teaching style

This is a long and complex case requiring two to three hours of class contact and a similar period of student preparation. Because of its length and the range of issues it covers, it is important to keep up a lively pace throughout. The topics are interdependent so students will have to prepare all the material even to answer only one aspect. For this reason, partial analysis of the case is NOT recommended. This case is best conducted in plenary.

Allow for plenty of blackboard space (or equivalent) and an overhead projector. Use the latter for displaying the organizational structure (1976) and add the changes with coloured pens during discussion.

The case inevitably provokes discussion on honesty in the workplace, so prepare some general questions relating to what individual students regard as acceptable behaviour in their own industries. Use the case as a scenario for interpersonal skills role play. 'Mars' (1983) introductory chapters make useful pre-class reading.

References

K. K. Back, *Assertiveness at Work*, (McGraw-Hill, 1982).

R. Bolton, *People Skills*, (Prentice Hall, 1979).

C. Handy, *Gods of Management*, (Souvenir Press, 1978).

A. Kakabadse, *The Politics of Management*, (Gower, 1983).

G. Mars, *Cheats at Work: Anthropology of Workplace Crime*, (Unwin, 1983).

T. J. Peters, and R. H. Waterman, *In Search of Excellence*, (Harper & Row, 1982).

E. Schein, *Career Dynamics: matching individual and organizational needs*, (Addison-Wesley, 1978).

SEVENTEEN

The Epicurus Leisure Group

SHAUN TYSON

Introduction

The problems facing the Epicurus Leisure Group in 1982 were similar to those experienced by much of British industry and commerce at that time. The issues raised are enduring however, and can be summarized under three headings.

1 How corporate planning and human resources planning are interrelated. Business planning is shown to be a broad activity which should involve a consideration of how to make the most productive use of the company's people assets as well as its financial assets.
2 How to develop a strategic view of managing change. The group's structure, its employee relations and management team, are key determinants in the successful management of change which this group faces as a result of the dramatic fall in demand for its major product.
3 The personnel policies which derive from marketing changes will be examined here, where the need to develop employee relations, training, and redeployment policies in order to support corporate initiatives, is explored.

Theory and background

The history of the group shows how successive technical innovations have ensured a continuing demand for television rental services. However, the sudden changes forecast indicate a failure by the board to realize the importance of introducing new products or services.

From this shock we might expect a re-examination of the whole corporate strategy.

Five steps are usual in corporate planning:

1 The corporate philosophy is defined.
2 Environmental conditions are scanned.
3 Corporate strengths, weaknesses, opportunities and threats are analysed (a SWOT analysis).
4 Objectives are derived from the analysis.
5 Strategies are developed to achieve the objectives.

At stage three there are a significant number of personnel strengths which contribute to the marketing choices available.

- Management and employees have expertise and experience in the marketing of domestic electrical and electronic equipment services.
- There is a widespread network of branches and service depots' together with a management structure in support.
- Epicurus Rentals has a good industrial relations record.
- The servicing team of 1000+ technicians is a reservoir of expertise which could be deployed in a number of ways, for example in the servicing of home computers.

There are many marketing opportunities available. The main choices are:

- Develop the existing business, especially contract rentals in hotels, second TVs at home etc.
- Move into new product areas, while continuing rental, such as home computers, video, entertainment centres, security systems.
- Offer retail sales with such products as television, 'white goods', videos etc.
- Undertake servicing of a wider range of products (e.g. home computers).

The relationship between the corporate plan and the human resource plan can be considered on these levels:

Corporate plan level: Strategic   –   Operational   –   Budget

HR plan level: Issues analysis   Forecasting demand   Action plans
                      (e.g. scenario planning)

The issues at the strategic level depend upon the marketing direction decided by the board. The important contribution to the strategic planning process is scenario planning, where a range of personnel options may be placed before the board, with a briefing on the likely consequences of following each path.

Key learning points

The human resource management issues which emerge at the strategic level are:

1   The need to reduce the number of staff in the representative, technician and headquarters categories, to reflect a changed set of priorities within the business. The historical labour turnover rate of 30 per cent p.a. may not remain constant, although some natural wastage will help reduce manning.
2   The retraining of technicians, to undertake appropriate work, for example the servicing of microcomputers.
3   The need to change the attitudes of staff at all levels to become used to a buyer's market.
4   Changes in roles for staff at all levels, as a consequence of the change from a single product to a multiproduct company.
5   The impact of change may bring to the fore any inherent conflicts between head office and regional staff.
6   Representatives duties could be handed over to the technicians in a renegotiation of the technician role.

   The management of the change process requires the development of a strategy in which any short-term actions are seen as compatible with long-term goals. Training activity in support of the changes should ensure:

1   The special training needs of middle managers and first line supervisors (for whom involvement in any change process is crucial), are met, so that they come to feel less vulnerable.
2   The development of an employee relations strategy which brings management, employees and trade unions together to support the corporate plan.
3   The promotion of personal counselling services, out placement counselling and similar schemes which help individuals through their transitions with less stress.

Personnel policies would also be required at the operational level in such areas as redundancies, reward structures and training, the precise nature of which are dependent on the strategic decisions taken.

Teaching guide summary

Issues	*Learning points*
1 Corporate planning/human resource planning interface.	• SWOT analysis of issues. • Personnel strengths create marketing opportunities. • Manpower planning links with corporate planning, through scenario planning.

2 Strategic management of change.	• Employee relations strategy including
	  employee involvement
	  new bargaining structures
	  communication techniques
	• Revised organization structure.
	• New management roles.
	• Training/development strategy.

3 Personnel policy changes.	• Personnel policies interlink. • Greater emphasis on employee development. • More flexible approach to rewards. • Redundancy, redeployment policies.

Teaching style

This case lends itself to a brainstorming approach to the solution of the marketing problems faced by Epicurus. When undertaking a SWOT analysis, the groups should be encouraged to look for the personnel strengths which will contribute to the corporate plan. After deciding the corporate plan in broad terms, a more detailed analysis should be sought in which the groups put forward alternative scenarios of human resource implications from the different marketing options. The time spent on this part should be limited to allow time for discussion of change strategies and personnel policies.

The remaining issues of how the changes could be managed should then be explored, by each group suggesting the overall approach to change it would adopt, and then describing the tactics of change.

Finally, a list of personel policies which would be required to support the marketing strategy should be drawn up.

References

D. J. Bartholomew, *Manpower Planning, Selected Readings*, (Penguin, 1976).

C. Brewster, and S. Connock, *Industrial Relations: Cost effective strategies* (Hutchinson, 1985).

S. Tyson, and A. Fell, '*Evaluating the Personnel Function*', (Hutchinson, 1986).

G. Zaltman, and R. Duncan, *Strategies for Planned Change*, (Wiley, 1977).

PART THREE

Personnel Planning and Systems

EIGHTEEN

Pallas Electronics

JOHN BERESFORD AND SHAUN TYSON

Introduction

This case is designed to illustrate the interaction between manpower supply and manpower demand forecasting. At the Bristol factory of Pallas Electronics there is a need to build up a trained labour force rapidly, while the factory is also under pressure to improve the output per person.

The case is useful for demonstrating how management need to understand what is happening in a given hierarchy of jobs by looking at the flows in and out. It shows how the differences between the labour turnover of new and existing employees upset a recruitment plan, and consequently the forecast levels of output were not achieved.

Theory and background

The management of Pallas have attempted to make major changes simultaneously. The new factory layout, and changes to production methods, together with a new bonus, have all been introduced at a time when the factory is recruiting a third more staff in order to fulfil a higher output target. As part of their planning, the managers have estimated labour turnover based on historical trends, as 20 per cent per annum.

The 'central' rate of labour turnover is usually calculated by the formula:

$$\frac{\text{total number of leavers in period} \times 100}{\text{average number employed during the period}}$$

The period is normally one year.

There is ample research evidence to show that labour turnover varies according to a number of factors, especially the age of employees and their length of service. Wastage rates are usually higher during the earlier part of service. Thus wastage curves typically are shaped as follows for groups of people.

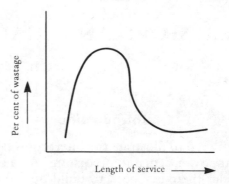

We know from the studies at Glacier metal that during the first few weeks of employment, employees suffer an 'induction crisis' before making a settled connection, and it is during this time that a higher wastage rate might be expected. To determine how the wastage rate varies, the personnel department should undertake a cohort analysis of the new recruits. Similarly the productivity of the new labour can be recorded, to differentiate their output from that of the existing staff. Such an analysis may then be used to evaluate the recruitment and training policies of the organization, and to adjust them accordingly.

Key learning points

1 Since wastage rates are known to be service specific, predictions of labour requirements must take the wastage of new and of existing staff into account. The rates are expected to be different. The period of the 'induction crisis' will vary and needs monitoring by means of a cohort analysis. As an example, the wastage rate for new staff estimated by the company was only 20 per cent p.a. As an example of a cohort analysis, the table below shows what a cohort analysis would look like.

Table 1 *End month composition of new labour by length of service in months*

Month	1	2	3	4	5	6	Numbers employed		
% loss	20	10	5	3	10	2			
Month Recruit							New	Base	Total
1	25	20						20	196	216
2	25	20	18					38	193	231
3	25	20	18	17				55	190	245
4	25	20	18	17	16			71	187	258
5	15	12	18	17	16	14		77	184	261
6	12	10	11	17	16	14	14	82	181	263

These figures cannot be derived from the case, but illustrate what
happened.

2   The productivity of new staff is unlikely to be as high as existing
staff. There is a need therefore to monitor and feedback this
information to those concerned with recruitment (to alter the
person specification if necessary) and with training (to create a
steeper learning curve if necessary). A table to illustrate what the
'base labour' could achieve is as follows:

Table 2

Month	Labour force utilization		
	'Base'	'New'	Base labour output
1	42	24	823
2	45	27	868
3	50	29	950
4	55	33	1028
5	58	34	1067
6	60	35	1086

3   The original plan was optimistic. The difficulties were experienced in trying to build a trained labour force in a short period of
time. Here we may note that management attempted to undertake
a series of changes simultaneously. This would have imposed extra
strains on the supervisors, who also had to cope with extra new
personnel. The training department was asked to train 100 new
people in six months at a time when the production system itself

was changing. We might expect an unsettling effect from the high labour turnover which would create greater difficulties. It is worth noting here that the new staff represented a very large proportion of those employed. Difficulties in training such numbers might be anticipated since there would be relatively few experienced workers available for both on-the-job training, and to maintain output.

4 Although we may be critical of the management for not foreseeing the likely difficulties associated with the recruitment of new staff, one important learning point is the difficulty of correcting a trend in a relatively short period of time. The position after six months requires action after the analysis. The identification of a pattern of leaving is useful for further projections. The numbers needed to maintain the quantity of labour at a level where the required production is maintained can be calculated, and the output figures for new and existing staff give a measure of how far short of the production target the company will be. The management then has a choice of either improving the recruitment flow, the training, trying to reduce wastage (by means of exit interviews), or adjusting the target.

Teaching guide summary

Issues	Learning points
1 Cohort analysis.	• Wastage is service specific.
	• The induction crisis.
	• Monitor the flows.
2 Productivity.	• Monitor productivity of the cohort.
	• Estimate productivity when calculating demand.
	• Feedback to training department.
3 Labour force build-up.	• Training of new staff disrupts production.
	• Effects on supervision.
	• Proportion of new staff to existing staff is significant.
4 Difficulty of correcting a trend.	• Monitoring, identification of a leaving pattern.
	• Exit interviews.
	• Projection of how labour will build up and adjust target accordingly.

Teaching style

The case is best handled by asking the groups to comment on the original plan first, and then to ask how they would seek to discover what had happened.

The students presenting their findings should be encouraged to draw up their recruitment plans on overhead projector transparencies, or on flipchart paper beforehand, and to explain the labour turnover assumptions behind their plans.

Tables 1 and 2 should be reproduced to show on the overhead projector, as an example of how a cohort analysis may be drawn up, and how output figures can be calculated related to the appropriate part of the workforce.

The discussion in the case can be directed at the end towards a consideration of how projections of the demand for labour is dependent on the supply side forecast.

Further reading

A. K. Rice, J. M. Hill, and E. L. Trist, 'The representation of labour turnover as a social process', *Human Relations*, 3, 1950, pp. 349–381.

H. Silcock, 'The phenomenon of labour turnover', *Journal of the Royal Statistical Society*, 1954, pp. 429–44.

A. Bowey, *A guide to manpower planning*, (Macmillan, 1973).

D. J. Bartholomew, '*Stochastic Models for Social Process*', (John Wiley and Sons, 1973).

Department of Employment, '*Company Manpower Planning*', Manpower Papers no. 1, HMSO, 1968.

W. Brown, and E. Jaques, *Glacier Project Papers*, (Heinemann Educational Books, 1965).

NINETEEN

Archon Engineering

SHAUN TYSON

Introduction

The divisional structure created for Archon Engineering poses the question, what kind of personnel role is suitable for the new divisional organization? In answering this question it is necessary to discover what the expectations of senior line managers are of the scope and function of personnel work, and how personnel can contribute to the division's business strategy. In this case, the divisional personnel manager's main task is to change the negative expectations held by the managers in the operating companies and to establish his own credibility with Robertson, the divisional general manager.

Theory and background

A number of researchers have commented upon the disparity between the apparent authority of personnel managers, and the actual power that they exercise (Ritzer and Trice 1969; Watson 1977). Their authority normally stems from lateral sources (Gross 1964). Ambiguity surrounds the role, where personnel managers may be perceived for example as a 'loyal opposition' devoted to the welfare of employees, as a means of controlling behaviour, or as a tactical response to trade union pressure. This leads to an ambiguity cycle:

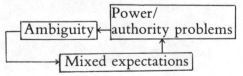

where the mixed expectations of the role feed the ambiguity of the role, which results in line managers being unwilling to accord personnel managers the authority they desire (Tyson 1980).

Personnel managers may make a number of responses to this problem. Legge (1978), suggests that the way they respond is contingent upon the organizational context. The conclusion we may draw from research is that the occupational purpose is to sum up the organization's personnel requirements, the often unexpressed expectations of personnel, in a coherent model of the personnel function which provides the level of service, and the contribution to the organization which senior managers require (Tyson 1983; Tyson and Fell 1986).

Three such models have been delineated.

1   The 'clerk of works' model, where personnel managers act in an administrative, supportive role, where resource acquisition and welfare are seen as the key variables on which the function is judged.
2   The 'contracts manager' model, where personnel managers are concerned mainly with the maintenance of systems and industrial relations procedures, in order to sustain harmonious relationships. In this model personnel specialists tend to react to line manager demands, and the issue on which personnel is judged is stable employee relations.
3   The 'architect' model, where personnel managers concentrate on designing policies, and on making strategic contributions to the corporate plan. This is an output model where personnel managers are evaluated on their contribution to profit increase or cost reduction, as part of organizational goals.

In the Archon Group, there are diverse requirements at the local level, and the divisional personnel manager has the difficult task of trying to discover which model of the personnel function is suitable for each organization, to see if sufficient commonality can be found within these company models to grant him a coherent divisional role.

To prevent Robertson from pulling the personnel function into his own political ploys, Jones needs to establish his credibility as a contributor to the business. Jones' effectiveness is not only dependent on his political interpersonal skills, but also on the way he creates a personnel model which can sum up the needs of each organization in the division.

Key learning points

The divisional personnel manager has made a useful start by identifying the main issues for each company. These can be summarized as follows:

The paint company

In this company, there are problems with the reward structure (no pay scales, no systematic review etc.), consequently there are dissatisfied managers and first line supervisors. This may become an industrial relations problem if ASTMS is successful in its recruitment campaign, and seeks to bargain with the company on behalf of the managers. The personnel department seems to be operated in a 'clerk of works' model, with inadequate systems and controls. The company has marketing problems and needs investment in new plant, but there is a corresponding need for management development, so that managers can be trained to cope with the transition to a more modern and professional approach. This would be consistent with the group's objectives.

Consumer products

In this instance, it is the absence of immediate personnel problems which gives rise to the question: what can a divisional Personnel Department offer to such a profitable company? Although the company has been profitable up to now, there are strategic issues which it needs to address. The 'clerk of works' model of personnel which prevails, implies that personnel issues are not seen as matters which influence the business. Yet the consumer products company is part of the fashion industry, and fashions by definition change. The future development of the business is highly dependent on both the quality of its marketing, the rapidity of its responses and the flexibility of its production. The dispersed factory locations and the part-time and sub-contract employees, while satisfying immediate needs, may not fit into its future requirements. This raises the issue of whether any corporate planning is undertaken, and how far the division and the group might be expected to underwrite future ventures.

The radiator company

The problems of the radiator company arise from a failure to operate satisfactory management controls over costs, and the tendency to regard harmony in relationships as a superordinate goal is a characteristic of the 'contracts manager' approach to personnel. Any advice from the Engineering Employers Federation would be unlikely to consider the long-term effects on profitability of this particular company (e.g. the divisional pricing policy), and the management's complacency here seems to require Jones to question the wisdom of the existing industrial relations strategy.

Summary

The divisional personnel function needs to follow the 'architect' model. This can be achieved by operating a consultancy service for the companies within the division, and designing a divisional personnel plan, to cover salary policy, the long term planning processes and industrial relations strategies. It is important to develop personnel policies which are in tune with the specific requirements of each business.

In the paint company, a local personnel department should be created which is initially on the 'contracts manager' model, but which can be moved as the immediate difficulties are overcome, into an 'architect' model. The personnel departments in the consumer products and radiator companies should be moved towards the 'architect' model, so that a more strategic vision of human resource management can be achieved.

At the divisional level, a division wide employee relations policy, management development policy, senior management reward policy, succession planning, and a broad policy on employee involvement and communications should be objectives for Jones, when the priorities at operating company level, outlined above, have been established.

Teaching guide summary

Issues	Learning points
1 Effectiveness.	• Personal effectiveness depends on gaining access to the decision-making caucus of the company. Effectiveness for the personnel department arises from its members being able to sum-up senior management requirements, and to deliver on these. This avoids the ambiguity cycle.

2 Models of personnel management.	• Three models: the 'clerk of works' clerical supportive 'contracts manager' systems, reactive architect, business manager.
3 Changing models.	• Operate at level of business needs. Prioritize requirements, using the appropriate model for immediate needs, whilst moving towards a wider approach.
4 Human resources strategy.	• Long-term strategic decisions needed to create employee relations strategy covering rewards policy, management development, communications, bargaining structures.

Teaching style

The case can be incorporated into a discussion on the role of personnel management, or may be used to illustrate the creation of personnel policies in a divisional structure. The presentations may be used to encourage a discussion of the interconnections between structure and policy, and should allow a debate on the models of personnel revealed by the case. One way of teaching the case is to ask those presenting the arguments for a stronger divisional personnel function to justify their position, under questioning from either the tutor or other class members taking Robertson's perspective. If different positions are taken by different groups within the class, these may be used to demonstrate the models of personnel typically held by members of the class.

Further reading

E. Gross, 'Sources of lateral authority in personnel departments', *Industrial Relations*, vol. 3, 1964, pp. 121–33.
K. Legge, *Power, Innovation and Problem Solving in Personnel Management*, (McGraw-Hill, 1978).
G. Ritzer, and H. M. Trice, *An occupation in conflict. A study of the personnel manager*, (Cornell University, 1969).

S. Tyson, 'Taking advantage of ambiguity', *Personnel Management*, February 1980.

S. Tyson, 'Personnel Management in its organizational context' in K. Thurley and S. Wood (eds), *Industrial Relations and Management Strategy*, (Cambridge University Press, 1983).

S. Tyson, and A. Fell, *Evaluating the Personnel Function*, (Hutchinson, 1986).

T. J. Watson, *The Personnel Managers*, (Routledge and Kegan Paul, 1977).

TWENTY

Lysander Products

SHAUN TYSON

Introduction

The reward structures at Lysander Products are no longer meeting the needs of the organization. The job evaluation system has fallen into disuse, there is no published guide to salary administration, and the management controls have ceased to be effective.

This is all within the context of falling demand for the company's main product which has brought a new general manager, whose brief is to improve the profitability of the company. The case is therefore suitable for examining the problems of updating reward structures at a time of financial constraint. A number of crucial decisions have to be made. These include: the choice of which job evaluation scheme, and the number of reporting levels of management. The constraints placed on the personnel manager – a short time scale and the restriction on extra money, also illustrate some of the problems found in a typical consultancy assignment.

Theory and background

Difficulties with reward structures often emerge because systems have not been maintained, or have become irrelevant to business needs. Job evaluation schemes do become out of date, and this can lead to cynicism among those to whom they apply. One symptom of failure is 'grade drift', where successive job regradings have occurred, so there is a disproportionate number of jobs in the higher grades. A further symptom of reward structure disorder is seen where the salaries actually paid have ceased to correspond to the official minima and maxima for the grades. These problems may emerge for a number of reasons, for example, due to rapid change, new methods, new technologies, due to weak personnel management, high labour turnover in skill shortage occupations, or because of a combination of these factors.

The relationship between effort and reward is structured by a system of rules and procedures which embody the organization's policies on salaries and wages. Salary policy objectives are typically concerned with:

- Remaining competitive for labour.
- Rewarding effort, providing an incentive for employees.
- Being felt to be fair by employees.
- Controlling employment costs.

There may also be broader questions of company philosophy or culture which influence reward policies, such as the harmonization of pay and conditions, or the use of reward policy to share rewards and give a measure of employee involvement.

Job evaluation schemes are introduced in order to help organizations to achieve the aims of their salary policies. The main reasons are:

1 Some form of job evaluation is necessary to introduce rationality into pay scales.
2 Job evaluation helps to determine how to change rewards if the job content changes.
3 Job evaluation enables comparisons to be made, both externally with other organizations, and within the organization between jobs on an explicit basis.
4 Most schemes require the establishment of job evaluation committees which in themselves are a form of participation.

There are four main types of job evaluation schemes. Schemes may be classified as either analytical or non analytical of job content. They are appropriate to different situations, as described below.

Non analytical schemes

Classification schemes are a form of organization design, and are most suited to those situations where jobs do not change rapidly, and where there is no technical content to the job.

Whole job ranking schemes which involve taking jobs as wholes and making very broad comparisons are suitable for a relatively small number of different jobs, and are not easy to use when new jobs appear frequently.

Analytical schemes

Factor comparison schemes come in a variety of forms, but are unpopular in the UK. Those which are regarded as 'direct to money' schemes rely on stability in wage rates for their efficacy, and those which just rank the factors suffer from the disadvantages of whole job ranking.

Points schemes are suitable for complex organizations and for a mixture of technical and non technical jobs and can be readily adapted to the requirements of particular organizations. However, complex proprietary schemes, such as Hay, are expensive and require sophisticated personnel functions to cope. On the other hand, tailor-made schemes take time to establish and require consultancy expertise to help create them.

Key learning points

The job evaluation scheme in Lysander is of the 'classification' type, but has clearly fallen into disuse. The organization charts show that responsibility levels are no longer expressed by the grade level. The general dissatisfaction with salaries, and the loss of face validity in the current scheme are undermining the existing approach to rewards. There seems to be no known reasons for the grades awarded to particular positions.

There is also the problem of the existing organization structure. The new general manager has been appointed with a brief to change the organization. He will no doubt wish to reduce the number of managers in the organization, and review the structure.

A further difficulty facing the new personnel manager is the time scale in which the solutions are being sought. The general manager's view of the problems and their solution is in need of modification. The problem will only be solved if an adequate job evaluation scheme is introduced, but that will take time, and is unlikely to be without cost – in extra salaries and in consultancy fees, and time and resources from the personnel department.

The options available either to the personnel manager, or to a consultant undertaking the assignment, can be summarized as follows:

1   Introduce a new scheme. The preferred type would be a points based scheme, which would be analytical of job content. The benefits of a points scheme are that it would be possible to cover the whole range of jobs without difficulty, and would adjust

more readily to new jobs, and to rapid change. This leaves the question of whether to design a tailor-made scheme which could be created to meet the specific circumstances at Lysander, or whether to bring in an off-the-shelf scheme, (for example the Hay system). This latter course would be quicker than a tailor-made scheme, but would be expensive. In addition to the consultant's fees, there would be the additional costs of training personnel and line management. The lack of expertise in the personnel department is a consideration. The time limit of six months would put pressure on the exercise but assuming there are approximately ninety different jobs, the completion of the scheme is attainable in time.

2　Make marginal changes to the existing scheme. This option would mean rewriting the classification scheme, showing the new levels of responsibility more accurately. This is potentially the quickest option and would have the benefit of drawing on existing knowledge and usage. However, the current scheme has fallen into disrepute, and the pace of change would make the old scheme increasingly irrelevant. This could not be seen as a good long term solution therefore.

3　Design a new classification scheme. This would imply reducing the number of grades and working with the general manager in order to design the new organization structure. Reducing the number of levels in the organization structure, together with corresponding grades would be a useful option given the overriding requirement to make the business more efficient. However, this implies that the organization will move to a new, static structure, which seems to be unlikely in the face of changes to products, and to likely future events. The new classification scheme would be useful, initially, but might soon prove to be inflexible, and would require further revision, with all the attendant costs and disruption.

To summarize the strategic position: the second and third options offer the opportunity for the strategic involvement of the general manager, but neither are likely to be a satisfactory lasting solution. In managing the changes, the personnel manager should consider a two stage approach: the involvement of the general manager in the redesign of the organization structure with an interim arrangement on the current grades to overcome anomalies and to make the salary review acceptable to the management team, followed by a new points scheme to be introduced over a longer period.

Teaching guide summary

Issues	*Learning points*
1 Reward policies help to create the organization culture.	• Employee involvement, felt fair pay, and motivational issues are implicit in reward policy.
2 Reward structures have strategic impact.	• Strategy for changing organizations frequently entails changing reward structure and the redesign of organization structures has a major impact on classification schemes.
3 Job evaluation helps to establish fairness, and employee involvement.	• Job evaluation seeks to establish an order for jobs to which all may agree. Jobs, not people, are evaluated.
4 Four main types of scheme: *Non-analytical* Classification	• Suitable for stable organizations. • Organization design involved.
Whole job ranking	• Suitable for small number of jobs, and for non-technical jobs.
Analytical Factor comparison	• Ranking of factors. Best for small number of jobs, or for similar categories (e.g. admin clerical etc.).
Points schemes	• Suitable for a variety of jobs and for rapidly changing environment. Complex, expensive to introduce and to maintain.
5 Pragmatic approach to change.	• Changes need to be seen in stages. Involvement of top management is essential for success. Immediate problems need to be solved before embarking on long-term solutions. Face validity important for new reward structures.

Lysander Products

Teaching style

This case is best taught after the main principles of job evaluation have been introduced in a mini lecture. It can be dealt with as a vehicle for classroom discussion or for more formal report back presentations, since the reason behind the decisions the personnel manager takes are as important as the decisions themselves. It is particularly useful to ensure that those advocating specific actions are able to explain how these would be implemented, so that consultancy style can come out of the debate – in addition to a technical knowledge of job evaluation.

Further reading

A. Bowey, *Handbook of Salary and Wage Systems*, (Gower, 1976).
B. Livy, *Job Evaluation: A Critical Review*, (Allen and Unwin, 1975).
S. Tyson, and A. York, *Personnel Management Made Simple*, (Heinemann, 1982), Chapters 15 and 16.

TWENTY-ONE

Thomas Nestor Limited

SHAUN TYSON

Introduction

Thomas Nestor Limited was a small printing company, which had to make major changes as a consequence of the recession. The purpose of this case is to examine the ways in which management development can help managers to adjust to change within their organization. The case can be taken at two levels: as a study of the relationship between organization development and management development, and as a vehicle for discussing techniques in management development. Although management development is often seen as appropriate in larger organizations, this case illustrates the significance of management development to smaller companies, even in very traditional industries such as printing.

Theory and background

Management development has been defined as a systematic process for creating effective managers, now and in the future. For many organizations the recession has created an urgent need for organizational learning to take place – i.e. for a major shift in attitudes, with greater business awareness, increased commitment, and the skills to cope with a wider range of tasks.

The process by which new behaviours come to be adopted is the process of learning. Management development can be seen as the term which covers all the ways in which this learning takes place. At the heart of the activity is a requirement to help managers to be able to learn. Often middle aged, sometimes frightened of change, such managers find adjusting to any formal or structured techniques difficult. Preparing managers explicitly to 'learn how to learn' is perhaps the most obvious first step. Without this step, the learning environment will not be created. The organization structure, and the personnel policies are a part of the environment, which should assist learning (Tyson 1984). Attention to the following policies to make learning an intrinsic part of all jobs is therefore necessary.

- Job design, to include built-in feedback on performance.
- Reward structures which encourage creativity and original thinking.
- Management style which encourages legitimate risk taking.
- Promotion policies which are open, and which work on clearly defined, merit based criteria.
- The development and coaching of subordinates as a recognized part of all supervisory jobs.

Management development strategy is therefore a part of the overall business strategy. To sustain, or maintain a business, managers must be able to adapt themselves, and to change others. The following issues will need consideration:

1 Which groups of managers should be involved in management development?
2 How will those people identified as possessing high potential be developed?
3 How to integrate the various technical, induction and training activities into a coherent training policy?
4 What mechanism will be used to identify training needs (e.g. appraisal reports, etc.)?
5 How to cope with very specific training requirements?
6 To what extent should the organization rely on internal resources, and which external bodies should be involved?
7 If 'trainers' are involved either as internal or external consultants, how should senior management liaise with them?
8 What kind of support is necessary to achieve corporate targets in all the main functions?

From the answers to these questions a broad development strategy will emerge. The activities which may be conducted as part of the development of managers will vary according to the identified needs, and typically range from on-the-job counselling, and coaching, to formal off the job development, such as sponsorship on an MBA programme.

Key learning points

The small family owned printers, Thomas Nestor, have successfully introduced major changes which have enabled them to cope with the recession. A small organization structure has been created, new technology has been introduced, and many of the old restrictive practices, so well entrenched in the printing industry, have been abandoned. All of this has been achieved in order to make the company more responsive to the demands of the market place, and to operate with a more competitive cost structure.

For the opportunities to be exploited there is likely to be a need for new behaviours within the management team. The development of a management strategy can thus be examined under the eight questions above.

1 *Groups of managers.* All the managers should be involved here, since one of the benefits of a total company approach will be to foster a strong company spirit.
2 *Identification of potential.* This is not a priority at Nestor but the training needs analysis might reveal those managers who have strong potential for further growth.
3 *Coherent training policy.* This means gaining agreement from the whole management team on the training activities, and creating a written policy showing the different aspects. This should also be shared with the unions, who may wish to have an input to the priorities in the policy.
4 *Identification of training needs.* The lack of adequate systems implies that a training needs analysis approach which uses assessment centre methodology (tests, exercises, case studies etc.) could be used as the first stage in the training process. Appraisal systems could be developed which routinely help to identify training needs.
5 *Specialist training requirements.* The use of outside courses should be considered for those who would benefit from exposure to other cultures, where the need is not general.
6 *Resources.* The absence of skilled trainers and the amount of work to be done results in the conclusion that the Personnel Director should hire expertise once the strategic issues have been decided.
7 *Involvement of senior management.* The first step towards an agreed approach will be for the Personnel Director and the Managing Director to present their ideas to the management team, and to have regular liaison meetings with them (including any outside experts who are engaged).

8   *Support for the business strategy.* In addition to any individual needs identified at the 'assessment' or 'development centre' the changing needs of the business are likely to require Nestor's managers in the future: to be more flexible, to be better communicators, to have a broad knowledge of marketing and finance, and to have the confidence to tackle new problems as they emerge.

The supporting systems created within Nestor should have the following objectives:

- They should be person centred, rather than problem centred.
- To increase the individual's propensity to learn.
- To improve their capacity as managers of the business.
- To give managers clear goals.
- Selection, promotion should be based on rational performance related criteria.

The techniques which might be considered after the training needs analysis are:

1   A series of modules, following the analysis at a 'development centre'

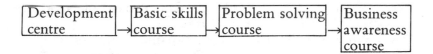

2   Projects – using action learning techniques, especially project teams across functional boundaries.
3   Attendance on senior management development courses (external) for the top team, in addition to above.
4   'Team-building' courses, including outdoor development to build confidence, and provide feedback from tutors on behaviours.
5   Horizontal transfers for those with high potential, in order to expose them to different parts of the business.

There would be benefits in forming a relationship with an outside body, such as a well known management training establishment or business school, to give the necessary help with these activities. The activities are not mutually exclusive – and could be assembled in appropriate mixes over a period of eighteen months. Regular review and feedback on the management development programme should include an evaluation of each event/activity against the agreed criteria for success.

Teaching guide summary

Issues	*Learning points*
1 Management development strategy.	<ul><li>Group managers according to need.</li><li>Identify potential.</li><li>Create coherent training policy.</li><li>Regularly identify training needs.</li><li>Cater for specialist training requirements.</li><li>Allocate resources.</li><li>Involve senior managers.</li><li>Support the business strategy.</li></ul>
2 Developmental approach.	<ul><li>Person centred, not problem centred.</li><li>Increase propensity to learn.</li><li>Clear goals needed.</li><li>Select/promote people on rational criteria.</li><li>Coaching part of supervisor role.</li></ul>
3 Developmental activities.	<ul><li>Tailor-made courses.</li><li>Off-the-job courses.</li><li>Action learning through projects.</li><li>Horizontal transfers.</li><li>Team building.</li><li>Development centres with feedback to participants.</li></ul>

Teaching style

Prior to tackling this case, students should be familiar with the broad issues of management development at a time of change. It is quite effective to ask the individuals or groups reporting to do so as if they were reporting to the board, or to a general meeting of managers and trade union representatives. The remaining members of the class may then cross question the reporter on the reasons behind each decision. The tutor should also ensure that a practical solution is advanced, with specific proposals for developmental activities.

Thomas Nestor Limited

Further reading

J. Burgoyne, T. Boydell, and M. Pedler, *A Manager's Guide to Self Development* (McGraw-Hill, 1978).
H. Hague, *Management Training for Real*, (IPM, 1973).
S. Tyson, 'Management Development as a part of Organization Development', *Management Monitor*, November 1984.
S. Tyson, and A. Fell, *Evaluating the Personnel Function*, (Hutchinson, 1986).

TWENTY-TWO

Recruiting a national sales force

FERGUS PANTON

Introduction

This case highlights some of the policy issues in recruitment and selection work; the systems and procedures involved and the potential interdepartmental and interpersonal behavioural problems that may arise.

Its most obvious use is to provide an opportunity to review the recruitment and selection process as a whole, and it could be included in any general management programme, personnel or management development course.

Theory and background

The recruitment and selection process

Before introducing the case, tutors may like to provide an overview of the total process which students can use as a guideline for their discussions.

There can be no simple answer to the question of how best to recruit and select people. One is trying to predict how individuals will behave in future situations under variable conditions. However, there is no doubt that the quality of the recruitment and selection process can be greatly improved, and costly mistakes reduced, if a systems approach is followed.

One such approach can be called WASP, an acronym for:

*W*orking out requirements:
manpower planning, job analysis, person specification.
*A*ttracting applicants:
company reputation, employment market, advertising.

Selecting applicants:
  screening, interviewing, short-listing, assessing.
Placing applicants:
  job design, induction, administration.

Key learning points

Questions raised

The questions posed in the case will, it is hoped, stimulate study groups to discuss both the practical problems facing the company and what principles, if any, were involved.

Notes on each question follow, as an aid to further discussion. (Numbers refer to the case study task.)

1   Who was going to brief the agencies? In what way?
The first of these questions raised the fundamental issue of where responsibilities for decision-making and action lay. There was a conflict of interests and mutual distrust between the sales department and the personnel department. Both 'sides' were brought together to clarify who, for each stage of the recruitment process, had prime or secondary responsibility for decision-making or even where it was shared. This went some way towards reducing unproductive conflict but it became evident later that the causes of friction were more deep-seated.

It was agreed that responsibility for the briefing and control of the agencies was personnel's, but that the requirements would be specified by sales and personnel would work to their specification.

2 and 6   The employment market
A frequent – and justified – cry from the recruitment agencies is that most conventional personnel practice in recruitment and selection spends insufficient time and consideration on one vital element – *attracting applicants.*

This was certainly true of ICG. No one, including the personnel specialists had clearly thought through what their source of supply would be, and if that is not known or planned how is the advertising to be planned?

What the consultant strived to obtain – without success – was a policy guide-line like:
1   We will recruit primarily from the industry.
2   The prime experience required is in f.c.m.g.
3   Knowledge and experience of the industry is desirable but secondary to selling skills and personal drive.

3   Career prospects

Research shows that what most people are looking for when they move jobs are better career prospects, more autonomy, greater utilization of talent. In other words, they look beyond the immediate job on offer to the future. Yet most companies are pre-occupied with analysing, defining and selling the particular job.

ICG was no exception, but, to be fair, the whole exercise was at a high risk premium and they felt it would be unethical to talk of career prospects. What they planned to do was to *give* career advancement, namely at each of the management levels they would recruit from the level below.

4 and 12   Working out requirements

There are no grounds for disputing 'the conventional personnel route of job analysis – job description – person specification'. Here, however, time was a critical factor, and the interdepartmental team, understanding the principles, was able to dispense with the well-tried but more laborious parts of the system and go straight to writing person specifications without any obvious adverse consequences. Further, agreement that the 'desirable' characteristics at one level could usefully comprise the 'essential' characteristics at the next higher level not only saved duplication of effort but ensured some continuity of standards.

5   Geographical knowledge

Knowing the district, the people – where they live, how they earn their money – is vital in selling. And it helps to be familiar with routes, forms of transport and logistics.

To get this particular project going it would have made sense to set recruitment targets like 'not less than 60 per cent of the staff taken on must have experience of 'x' years work in the region/area'. This was not done in a formalized way, although local knowledge was favourably reviewed in the final selection.

Interestingly it became evident that the North/South split in England was a factor in determining the probable acceptability of sales persons and there was much support for the theory of Scots for Scotland and Welsh for Wales.

7   Women

This was a traditionally male dominated area of employment, whether by male choice or female disinterest was unknown. Some, but very few, women applied: some were appointed. There was no policy. Should there have been?

8 and 9   Conditions of employment
The first substantial interviewing programme was for potential regional managers. Although the interviewers were fairly confident that they had short-listed the best of the candidates, the final selection panel rejected all but one because they did not consider them to be of sufficient calibre. This in retrospect was good thinking, but it was not exactly highly motivating for the two selection teams that had done all the donkey work especially as it cast doubt either on their skill or on the system, or on both. A critique session between sales and personnel exposed one of the principal hang-ups, which had not been adequately confronted before, and this was on the fundamental issue of remuneration levels.

The sales manager maintained that they were pitched too low and would not attract good enough candidates. The personal manager suspected that the argument was a ploy to get all sales salaries increased, was concerned about relativities in the company as a whole and struggled to maintain the status quo. It was a conflict of roles and value systems and it was 'resolved' in the most common manner – by a mixture of power politics and compromise. The jobs were readvertised, this time under the company's name, with an increased salary offer, and the second time round there was a very marked improvement in the quality of the candidates who presented themselves – but what did that prove?

What had become apparent was that if applicants were to be attracted from the industry, there had to be an immediate financial inducement as well as enhanced career prospects. To illustrate, grade 1 sales representatives in competitive companies were found to be earning as much – and in some cases more – as it had been planned to offer area managers. Fringe benefits and allowances were also comparable, so there was no room for manoeuvre.

It took courage to resolve the vexed question of remuneration levels, because considerable sums of money were at stake. It was the Personnel Director who decreed that 'salary should not be the excuse for not obtaining the right people'.

During interviews it became very clear that sales staff attached great importance to the kind of car that went with the job and mileage allowances etc. They showed little interest in other conditions of service, although there was a very beneficial pension scheme and other fringe benefits.

10, 11, 13 and 14   Selecting
The experience gained in the first abortive round of interviewing led to several important policy decisions.

- Two two-man selection teams were set up, each comprising a sales and personnel manager who interviewed as a panel.

    They travelled extensively for six weeks 'on the trot' interviewing an average of five candidates a day for four days – a gruelling experience.
- The regional managers would be selected first and they would be actively involved in selecting their area managers who in turn would be involved in selecting representatives where possible.
- Group selection procedures, or assessment centre techniques, would be used for all managerial appointments. They would last for 1.5 days and be held in hotels in London. Eight candidates would be invited to each board and an average of four appointments would be made from each board. Therefore at the interviews one was in effect producing a short list of two for each job.

    Altogether eleven group selection boards were held in a space of three weeks. They consisted of individual and group tasks performed in front of three selectors.

    In general, they served their purpose well by providing an opportunity for candidates to be compared with each other, in circumstances that called for a wider range of behaviour than the interview. To some extent they tested stamina and persistence and gave an indication of interests and motivation which could not be so readily determined at an interview.
- In addition to group selection procedures, two verbal selection tests were used to provide complementary information, one 'intelligence' and one 'personality'.

Teaching guide summary

1 Anyone involved in selection work is also implicated in manpower planning. If manpower planning is not effectively conducted, recruitment and selection will fail.
2 It is essential to carry out a thorough and comprehensive survey of all economic conditions relating to the employment market – and one must know the target population for recruitment before this can be done.
3 It is essential that joint training of the employing department and of personnel is carried out. Personnel ought to have the skills but almost certainly lack job knowledge. The employing department is likely to lack skills – though convincing them may take time and skill.

4 The two-person joint interviewing team is economic and can be very effective.
5 Interviewing is an exhausting activity, both mentally and physically. To a salesperson who is always on the move, it looks easy until the person is exposed to the much more rigorous and less superficial discipline than normally experienced.
6 Selection boards earned their keep, especially when linked with selection tests. Both provided useful data to corroborate or otherwise interview judgements.

Teaching style

The approach indicated at the conclusion of the case, was that the class would address a long list of questions, designed to explore many of the issues raised when a recruitment exercise is undertaken. The style of teaching recommended is that the class should be encouraged to continue the discussion so that the benefits of examining any recruitment task under the broad headings contained in the notes is revealed. There are clearly no firm answers to the questions, but the reasons for the answers given by the class should be fully explored to see if they understand the pitfalls and opportunities of the selection process.

Further reading

P. Herriot, *Down from the Ivory Tower*, (John Wiley, 1984).
G. and H. Jessup, *Selection and Assessment at Work*, (Methuen 1975).
C. Lewis, *Employee Selection*, (Hutchinson, 1985).
R. Plumbley, *Recruitment and Selection*, (IPM, 1971).

PART FOUR

Employee Relations

TWENTY-THREE

East Midland Electronic

ROGER JONES

Introduction

The East Midland Electronic case describes and analyses the control systems, both formal and informal, found in an electrical equipment manufacturing company which employed about one thousand people. These control systems included budgetary, production control, payment and quality control systems. The description of each department shows how these systems were manipulated and sometimes subverted by shop floor workers, supervisors, and managers in the organization, not due to any pathological desire by those concerned to create an inefficient company, but rather because the systems themselves were remote from the reality of the work performed.

Theory and background

Several studies show how particular formal controls like payment systems and budgets are manipulated. This leads to the question why does this happen to control systems? There are a number of possible explanations; the four main sets of theories are:

The sociotechnical systems approach

Since the studies undertaken at Western Electric's Hawthorne works informal work group norms and work group needs have been shown to be significant. A number of researchers have tried to show that it is the mismatch between the 'technical' system (or the 'task system') and the social system in the plant which brings about the dysfunctional behaviours (Miller and Rice 1967; Emery and Trist

1965). These ideas draw on a mixture of functional doctrine and systems theory to augment an explanation based on social and personal needs. Solutions according to this approach would be to find ways of adjusting the task and controls to suit the social system, through job redesign for example.

The social action interpretation

Writers in this tradition base their explanations on the way groups of people interact, on the strategies they pursue and on the meanings which the actors invest in each situation (Silverman 1970). A research study which is very similar to this case is reported by Roy (1955) who spent a year using participant observation methods in a machine shop to discover the strategies followed by work groups, the alliances they formed, their collusion and conflicts in a detailed explanation of what the situation meant for the 'actors' in the real–life drama. The rules of work which management elaborated in its attempt to control behaviour were reinterpreted by groups and individuals according to their definitions of the situation. Resistance to managerial controls was often seen to be necessary in order to get work done.

Explanations in terms of the power of the participants

If we accept this perspective, the struggle for control between management and workers is a struggle for power. In this case, power to control behaviour, and power over information derive from the control systems. The struggle is for power over resources. Edwards and Scullion (1982) for example, argue that the frontiers of control between management and work people are under continuous negotiation, and therefore move backwards and forwards as each side marginally gains the initiative. Two possible solutions would present themselves under this interpretation. Either management could gain more power and enforce its rules more ruthlessly, or the collective power of the shop floor workers could be channelled into work group problem solving approaches, with management adopting an individualistic philosophy.

The four orders of administration

In 1977, Jones and Lakin put forward a theory which explained why control systems fail, as in this case study. They argued that formal control systems tend to be based on abstract premises which do not pay sufficient regard to the empirical characteristics of enterprises. There is, therefore, a mismatch between the controls and the operations to which they are ostensibly applied. This is so obvious that it is, paradoxically, difficult to see. In the interests of efficiency it becomes necessary to separate control systems from actual operations. This separation results in self-contained administrative departments which respond to their own internal logic rather than to the operational requirements of the enterprises they serve. Jones and Lakin referred to administration of this kind as 'second' and 'third order'. Meyer and Rowan (1977) call this phenomenon 'ceremonial administration', where accountants produce 'shadow prices' 'they assume that given organizational units are necessary and calculate their value from their prices in the world outside the organization. Thus modern accounting creates ceremonial production functions and maps them on to economic production functions'. Efficiency is served, they argue, if ceremonial units and procedures are 'decoupled' from actual operations. The manipulations described in the case study illustrate how this decoupling is accomplished.

Key learning points

Informal systems

The case shows how within each department informal systems exist. The interplay of piecework and budgetary controls resulted in a situation where both supervisors and operators gained through the relaxation of job times. In the stores the formal system was quite inadequate, and there were attempts by operators and by storemen to devise their own informal system to improve efficiency.

Work group solidarity

There was widespread manipulation of the payment system, and clock card fiddles. The composition of the work groups was stable. Groups bargained about the distribution of work and of overtime. Groups collaborated over the hours worked which gave a common time to each individual's actual hours and hence consistent bonus earnings.

Supervisors and work groups collaborated to manipulate the systems

Supervisors condoned the 'piecework fiddles'. Output rather than quality was sought. Where faults occurred, culpability was widely distributed, as in the disputes between the drawing office and machine shop. The machine shop supervisors were able to avoid cost penalties because they had negotiated generous waste provision, and the supervisors sometimes had to argue with ratefixers for better timings to avoid errors. There was joint manipulation of budgetary control and of the payment systems.

Conclusion – Control systems not consistent with reality

Because assembly shops were at the end of the line they had to correct the faults of other departments. Payment and budget systems were 'manipulated' to reflect this fact. Production schedules were regarded as obsolete, and inspection had only a ceremonial value. In practice inspectors rarely used their power to stop a bonus payment because they needed cooperation of the operators. There was a conflict between production and quality control.

In summary, two conditions are required for a control system to work reasonably well: first, it must be consistent with the empirical features of the organization or department to which it applies, and second it must be intelligible to those who operate it. These conditions are unlikely to be met when the system is designed and installed either by outside consultants or by specialised administrators. Ideally, a control system should be designed by those who use it.

Teaching guide summary

Issues	Learning points
1 Manipulation and failure of formal control systems.	● Four theories of behaviour to explain: sociotechnical system – mismatch between task and social system social action – explanations in terms of strategies and meanings of actions Power – Struggle for power over resources dependent on group solidarity, different interests, management, work people Four orders of administration – Control systems remote from empirical

	reality; part of ceremonial administration.
	Decoupling of system from actual operations characteristic of third, fourth order administration.
2 Control systems not consistent with reality.	• Informal systems. • Work group solidarity. • Supervisors, work groups collaborate to manipulate the systems.

Two conditions for control systems to achieve objectives

1 Must be consistent with empirical features of organization.
2 Should be intelligible to those to whom it is to apply.

Teaching style

This case fits well with the case on piecework bargaining. It takes the discussion of manipulation into the realm of organization theory. It could thus be used to discuss informal versus formal systems, and also could be taken to illustrate different explanations of organization behaviour. There are no special instructions for handling the feedback from the class, although teachers may wish to ask the class to concentrate on particular departments.

Further reading

C. Argyris, 'Human Problems with budgets', *Harvard Business Review*, February 1953.

P. K. Edwards, and H. Scullion, *The Social Organization of Industrial Conflict*, (Basil Blackwell, 1982).

F. E. Emery, and E. C. Trist, 'The Causal Texture of Organizational Environments', *Human Relations*, 18, 1965, pp. 21–32.

G. H. Hofstede, *The Game of Budget Control* (Tavistock, 1968).

R. S. Jones, and C. F. Lakin, The Four Orders of Administration, *Management Decision*, Summer 1977.

R. S. Jones, and C. F. Lakin, *The Carpetmakers*, (McGraw-Hill, 1978).

T. Lupton, *On the Shop Floor* (Pergamon Press, 1963).

J. W. Meyer, and B. Rowan, 'Institutionalised Organisations: Formal Structure as Myth and Ceremony', *American Journal of Sociology*, September 1977.

E. J. Miller, and A. K. Rice, *Systems of Organisations: The Control of Task and Sentient Boundaries*, (Tavistock, 1967).

S. J. Rawin, 'The Manager in the Polish Enterprise: A study of accommodation under conditions of role conflict', *British Journal of Industrial Relations*, March 1965.

D. Roy, 'Efficiency and "the Fix": informal intergroup relations in a piecework machine shop', *American Journal of Sociology*, vol. 60, 1955.

D. Silverman, *The Theory of Organisations*, (Heinemann, 1970).

TWENTY-FOUR

A case of piecework bargaining

ROGER JONES

Introduction

This study of an aircraft manufacturing plant is set in the 1950s. It describes group behaviour, and the influence of payment systems. The case concerns the strategies used by management and workers to gain control over the effort/reward bargain, and shows how output restriction is used as a rational device by workers, in their attempts to maintain stable earnings and to maximize their income under a piecework payment system.

Theory and background

Much research evidence (Taylor, Marriott, Roethlisberger and Dickson, Roy, Lupton etc.) suggests that given the choice between expending more effort to increase income and withholding effort with a loss of income, workers will not always, or even usually, take the first choice.

'Limitation' or 'restriction' of output implies that workers adopt standards which fall below their physical and mental capabilities. There usually seems to be a point beyond which an offer of extra money does not induce extra effort.

The expression 'output limitation' is also used in the sense that workers' effort standards fall short of those thought to be appropriate by managers. Research reported by Tannenbaum suggests that senior managers have higher expectations than middle managers about what constitutes an appropriate work standard. The expectations of first line supervisors tends to be lower than middle managers but higher than workers. Actual standards coincide with the expectations of workers.

There seems to be four main kinds of explanation for output limitation:

1 The first attributes it to idleness or moral back-sliding, which are often thought to be especially characteristic of the working classes. This explanation was favoured by Taylor.

2 The second attributes output limitation to an absence of proper managerial controls. According to this view, the remedy for limitation is a technical matter of scheduling, controlling work flow, setting scientific work standards, proper training and selection, accurate job selection, equitable payment structures, and so on. In this case, the operator's discretion in his job must be minimized, and his performance regulated by close supervision.

3 The third explanation rests upon the findings of social scientists and relates to the functioning of work groups. One inherent function of these groups is supposed to be that of setting norms. According to this view, rate busters or 'teararses' are not responding to financial incentives; rather are they rejecting the social standards of their workmates. This is sometimes known as the 'human relations' approach. The kind of norms that are set, it is argued, are dependent on the administrative and supervisory environment, which can be hostile, threatening and unpredictable, and the norm will be protective and, hence, in management's view, restrictive. If the group perceives the environment to be supportive and predictable, the norms will be more susceptible to influence by management. One important difficulty here is that work environments are not usually that benign.

4 Fourth, another theory explains limitation of output as the product of a complex interaction among people in organizations, influenced by broad social and economic forces. The factors at play in these interactions are said to be as variable as the situations in which the interactions take place. This complex type of explanation stresses external influences which are either minimized or ignored by explanations 2 and 3. In particular, union organization and group cohesion together can cushion workers from the effects of adverse economic forces. In circumstances where labour is plentiful and there is much unemployment, group enforcement of wage-effort relationships may enable workers to withhold effort so as to make the job last longer.

Key learning points

The effort/wage or work/wage bargain

Contracts of employment between employees and an employer cannot be as precise as those between the buyer and seller of a consumer or capital good. Such a contract may specify that an employee works for an organization in a particular capacity during stipulated periods but, normally, it will not contain an exact description of the amount of work required. Much of this will, of course, be unknowable or unspecifiable. There will, therefore, be great scope for bargaining about the relationship between effort and reward.

In this aircraft plant, the piecework guarantee was interpreted as the agreement between the rate fixer and the operator. Piecework prices were subject to collective action because they had significance for the whole department, for example in the sheet metal shop, the senior shop steward had to sanction the agreed price.

It is likely that an employee on a fixed wage will have a radically different idea from his employer as to the amount of effort that is reasonable to expect for that wage. To the extent that an individual is free to do so, he will probably try to bargain so as to obtain, from his point of view, a more favourable effort-wage relationship. Further, he is likely to think that effort above a certain level is not worth any amount of money.

Hence the attitude exhibited by Ginger and Stan, and some of their colleagues towards overtime.

The piecework fiddle

The relationship between effort and reward is explicit under payment by results systems. The defects of piecework as a system have been discussed by W. Brown in *Piecework Abandoned* who argued for measured day work. However, neither this nor any other system of payment escapes from the influence of effort-wage bargaining. A good description of a 'piecework fiddle' can be found in the study of a transformer shop in Lupton's book, *On The Shop Floor*.

By using their initiative to find ways to improve the modification on the bomb-bay, Stan and Ginger were able to build up time in credit on this modification job, which they could use on some of the more urgently timed work.

Piecework strategies

Typical of the 'piecework fiddle' are the following stratagems which are demonstrated by Stan and Ginger, and their workmates, in their continual struggle with the rate fixer.

1 Going slow on untimed work on jobs which carry provisional times.
2 Not exceeding a certain level of earnings so as to protect oneself from rate cutting or a tightening of future job times.
3 Maintaining the maximum level of 'allowed' earnings by working on good and bad jobs.
4 Obtaining at least a 'fair' share of good jobs.
5 Continual and, if possible, collective harrassment of rate-fixers.
6 Exploiting every opportunity to obtain special and contingency allowances.

Impact of piecework systems on collective action

The effort-bargain will also, it can be argued, be influenced by broad economic influences. A shortage of labour will not only raise wages, but it will also tend to lower the amount of effort or work which an employer can obtain for a given wage. The results of effort bargaining will depend to a large extent on the collective power behind the individual. Workers who are well organized and who are members of cohesive work groups, will be more powerful than the less well organized in a given set of labour market conditions.

Although the collective controls over piecework earnings were not strong in the fuselage shop, the feelings over what the general level of bonus should be were exerting an influence over behaviour, which was also conditioned by the wing shop, where a closed shop had achieved a much higher average bonus level. Union membership was increasing.

Explanations in non-attitudinal terms

Certain difficulties arise when one attempts to explain output restriction in terms of individual attitudes. Some theorists seem to assume that people who express favourable attitudes towards work in general, and their jobs in particular, will be more efficient and diligent than those who express less favourable or unfavourable attitudes. Research, however, shows that behaviour and attitudes are frequently inconsistent. Often an individual's work performance may be determined more by group pressures than his attitudes.

Further problems occur because attitudes cannot, or should not, be measured on a linear scale. For example, a person may report that he obtains satisfaction from responsibility but at the same time he may say that he is satisfied by a job with minimal responsibilities. A person is likely to have a number of inconsistent attitudes.

The behaviour of the workers described in this case history can be seen to be entirely rational, and not to be a consequence of any deviant attitude. The piecework system encouraged the view that workers should seek to maximize their earnings, and in practice, that is what they sought to do. Their behaviour was also conditioned by the prevailing group norms, and by their own view of a 'fair rate'.

Teaching guide summary

Issues	*Learning points*
1 Output restriction.	• Four explanations: idleness of workers inadequate management controls work group cohesiveness complex interaction – social/economic forces at local level, and external forces.
2 Effort/wage or work/wage bargain.	• Subject to bargaining. • Rational for workers to maximize earnings. • Strategies for obtaining higher/stable earnings. • Using 'good' jobs to compensate for difficult jobs. • Protecting earnings by working to norms. • Dominance over rate fixers. • Exploiting special allowances. • Obtaining 'fair' share of good jobs.
3 Piecework and collective action.	• Collective power of workers. • Group cohesion significant. • Piecework evokes a collective response.

4 Behaviour consequence of multiplicity of variables.	<ul><li>Attitudinal explanation insufficient.</li><li>Economic/social conditions important.</li><li>Attitudes not linear.</li><li>Consistency and rationality has to be judged from workers' viewpoint.</li></ul>

Teaching style

The case study may best be taught as a part of a general introduction to group behaviour/payment systems/industrial relations. Students may well express strong value positions and it is helpful to ask students initially to concentrate on the learning about reward structures, and then to see how reward structures influence industrial relations. Presentation of the different positions – Stan and Ginger, management, the rate fixer etc. by different members of the class may help to bring out the underlying issues, and the values of the students.

Further reading

W. Brown, *Piecework Abandoned*, (Heinemann, 1962).

T. Lupton, *On the shop floor*, (Pergamon, 1963).

R. Marriott, *Incentive Payment Systems*, (Staples Press, 1957).

F. J. Roethlisberger, and W. J. Dickson, *Management and the Worker*, (Harvard, Cambridge, Mass, 1939).

D. Roy, 'Efficiency and the Fix', *American Journal of Sociology*, 60, 1954, pp. 225–66.

F. W. Taylor, 'The Principles of Scientific Management', (New York, 1913).

TWENTY-FIVE

BIFU: a problem of union structure and democracy

PAUL WILLMAN

Introduction

BIFU is a medium-sized, white collar union. It is growing, but the future of growth is uncertain both because there are competitive forms of staff representation and because the future size and composition of the financial sector is uncertain. In addition, growth has set up certain internal political strains, and generated a hybrid structure.

The case is thus useful for analysing the forces influencing trade union growth, structure and government, as well as the interaction between them. This analysis is pursued on a *disaggregated* level, i.e. it is concerned with the development of a strategy by trade union leaders rather than with the exogenous forces which might determine the overall level of union membership.

Theory

The case focuses on the distinction between *open* and *closed* unionism (Turner 1962). The types are distinguished *inter alia* by their orientation to potential membership, closed unions restricting access to certain defined groups, open unions looking for an expansion in their 'job territory' i.e. 'that area of the labour market where a union aims to recruit and retain membership' (Undy *et al.* 1981). BIFU moves during the period under consideration from an organization seeking only to recruit bank employees to one which has expanded its job territory to include the entire financial sector.

A central issue concerns the factors which caused this change of policy. Many writers have focused either on exogenous or personality factors in considering job territory changes. Turner (1962) sees such changes as following from changes in the industrial distribution of the occupations or skills on which the union has focused recruitment. Commons (1919) sees an expansion in the scope of recruitment as an attempt to retain control over a particular *product market*. On the other hand, Undy *et al.* (1981) see such changes purely in terms of the personal ambitions of union leaders. All of these are relevant in the BIFU case, but there are two additional factors:

1 Financial constraints pointing to a need for higher levels of membership to generate adequate subscription income (i.e. BIFU has a minimum efficient scale).
2 Competitive pressures from other staff representative bodies, particularly for mergers with small staff associations.

The case also focuses on the *mechanisms* through which growth occurs. Undy *et al.* distinguish:

1 'Merger' growth, involving legal transfers of membership effected by the union leaderships themselves; these are facilitated by decentralized or sectional structures which allow the incoming groups of members to retain identity and autonomy within the merged union.
2 'Natural' or 'non-merger' growth which divides between:
   (a) 'Received' growth, such as that resulting from employment expansion in the job territory or favourable legislation.
   (b) 'Achieved' growth, such as that resulting from policy changes or from successful recruitment campaigns.

BIFU has a job territory in which employment is expanding and will 'receive' growth. It can 'achieve' growth and succeed in merger activity to the extent that its structure becomes sectionalized and it pursues policies which are attractive to potential members. However, its 'merger market' involves both clearing bank staff associations and those elsewhere in the financial sector. It is unlikely to be able to succeed with the same policies in both.

The case raises questions about the appropriate structure for the union. Historically it relied on an area structure, and on full-time officials, rather than lay representatives. This made good sense where the largest banks were regional and in the absence of a reliable office representative structure. The merger waves of the 1960s left the union confronting the 'Big Four' banks, i.e. Barclays, Lloyds, Midland and Natwest. The favourable legislative climate of the 1970s allowed the development of office representative networks in some banks. Both the area structure and the reliance on full-time officials were called into question.

The newer sectional structure is appropriate to a financial sector 'segmented' between retail banks, finance houses, insurance etc. It also corresponds to the ambit of control of the senior full-time officials, each of whom would have his own section. However, it makes no sense in terms either of the ownership structure or the structure of collective bargaining in the industry (see Appendix 6 of case study). The ownership structure is still dominated by the 'big four'. Bargaining is primarily by *institution* but most members still work for a major clearer or one of its subsidiaries. The prospect of some combination of regional and 'trade-group' structure, similar to the TGWU, may be considered.

Key learning points

The major points to bring out in the case are:

1   The nature of unions as organizations, operating under financial constraints and in the face of competition from other organizations. Like other forms of organization, they experience internal and structural problems associated with growth.
2   Unions may expand their job territories under different sets of circumstances. The BIFU case shows a union compelled to expand the job territory in order to achieve minimum efficient scale.
3   Both the potential for expansion and the appropriate internal structure are influenced by changes to the pattern of ownership within the industry.
4   Policy determination depends on the interplay between power groups within the union, in this case the three major competing interests are those of the clearing bank membership, the full time officials and the General Secretary.

There are essentially three options open to the general secretary. The costs and benefits of each are listed below.

1   Revert to the area structure, focus on the CBU merger and seek no new members outside the clearing banks.

This approach would gain strong support from the clearing bank members and thus would be relatively easy to push through the executive and conference as presently composed. It would alienate the full-time officials, particularly if there were redundancies among them. If successful, it would almost double the union's membership through merger and would solve the long-standing problem of the union's identity. Merger opportunities outside banking would be lost, as might current members in those areas. There remains the question of the separate identity of the clearers; current trends in the financial sector suggest that this approach would focus on only part of the product market.

2 Go for full sectionalization, and the pursuit of members outside the clearers.

This would get the support of the full-time officials, and would probably lead to achieved and merger growth in non-banking areas. It would consolidate the position of BIFU as the union for financial service workers, having membership in all parts of the sector. However, it will experience considerable political opposition within the present structure and may scare the CBU off completely. Members may be lost in the clearers. Finally, it may not be appropriate for the structure of the industry.

3 Promote a hybrid system of areas and trade groups, each with representational rights on the executive.

At worst, this might alienate both camps, reducing growth prospects both within and without the clearing banks. At best, it might offer the compromise both camps seek. It would be easier to steer through current rule-making bodies than more radical change, although the duties and powers of area and trade groups would be the subject of disagreement. Most importantly, the hybrid structure would offer sectional or institutional organization for collective bargaining purposes while the area base would avoid the problem of the union becoming simply a loose federation of staff associations in different companies.

Teaching style

The case is appropriate for students who have already dealt with the basic problems of union growth and structure, and who are acquainted with the issues involved in studying union democracy. One possible schedule is:

15–20 minutes Lecture on trade unionism in the financial sector, introducing NUBE and BIFU and the problem of the staff associations.

30 minutes Group work on the case. Access to the rule book might be useful at this point.

45 minutes   Main group discussion of the major issues.
15 minutes   Closing lecture on the main learning points.

References

H. Clegg, *The Changing System of Industrial Relations in Great Britain*, (Blackwell, 1979), Chapter 5.

J. Commons, 'American Shoemakers 1648–1895; A Sketch of Industrial Evolution', *Quarterly Journal of Economics*, November 1919.

T. Morris, 'Inter union competition in the Clearing Banks' *Industrial Relations Journal*, vol. 17, no. 2, 1986.

H. A. Turner, *Trade Union Growth, Structure and Policy*, (Allen and Unwin, 1962).

R. Undy, *et al. Change in Trade Unions; The Development of UK Unions since 1960*, (Hutchinson, 1981).

TWENTY-SIX

Greenfield Industrial

PAUL WILLMAN

Introduction

Greenfield are an American company seeking to penetrate the EEC market for a particular type of motor component. They have no strong commitment to a particular location, nor do they have a global policy on trade union recognition. However, the Managing Director has formed a negative view of industrial relations in the UK, particularly in the car industry, based on hearsay rather than analysis. The case offers the opportunity for such analysis by asking for a consultant's report. The research for this report encourages students to focus on the comparative position of UK industrial relations within the EEC and on changes in the UK industrial relations climate since 1979.

Background

Companies differ in their industrial relations strategies. Some are avowedly non-union, some have systematic policies towards union recognition and some, like Greenfield, are more pragmatic, recognizing where they see advantages in it and remaining non-union where they do not (Purcell and Sisson 1983). The non-union option is favoured by a number of successful US firms (Foulkes 1980), some of whom operate in the UK, but none of whom are in the car industry. Greenfield, unconstrained by global policies, is in a position to decide on a UK policy on the balance of advantages.

There is now substantial evidence on the industrial relations policies of foreign owned companies in the UK (Buckley and Enderwick 1985). Foreign-owned firms tend not to join employers' associations, and any bargaining with unions takes place at plant or company level. There is also information available on working patterns on Greenfield sites (IDS 1984), particularly the introduction of group-working. Finally, there is the example of Nissan, which has operated a distinctive industrial relations policy at Washington, involving a single union deal with the AEU (Industrial Relations Review & Report (IRRR 1985): also see IRRR 1984 for some examples of other single-union deals).

There have been substantial changes since 1979 in industrial relations in the car industry. Employment has contracted, new working practices have been introduced and the strike rate has reduced substantially (Marsden *et al.* 1985; Willman 1984). This has reflected increasingly competitive conditions in the industry, particularly within the EEC. Several firms are overtly following perceived Japanese practice in man-management, including the reduction of demarcation and the introduction of teamwork (Marsden *et al.* 1985). Trade union reaction to this has been relatively low key since the high strike rates of the early 1980s. The car firms have not sought to remove trade unions from their plants, but rather to modify the way in which they operate (Willman and Winch 1985).

This is one of the key points for Greenfield, should it decide to recognize a trade union, since the car firms' example shows that management control can be lost to shopfloor unions and subsequently regained only at considerable cost. The recognition decision thus has to be underpinned by a strategy for the maintenance of control through collective bargaining. Following Purcell (1979) this strategy might include:

1 The encouragement of union membership and support for the closed shop where appropriate.
2 The encouragement of membership participation in trade unions.
3 The encouragement of inter union cooperation (where relevant).
4 The institutionalization of irreducible conflict.
5 The minimization of areas of unavoidable conflict.
6 The maximization of areas of common interest.
7 The reduction in power of strategic groups.
8 The development of effective control systems. The consultant's report should include suggestions as to how this control might be achieved.

Similarly, if the proposal is for a non-union plant, the report should focus not only on the issue of recruitment of a non-union workforce, but also on the *maintenance* of a union-free environment and the necessary long term *preventative* policies (Foulkes 1980).

Key learning points

1 The case introduces students to the industrial relations issues faced by inward investors in such a way as to enable comparison of the UK climate with those of other EEC countries.
2 It focuses on the role of inward investors, particularly on Greenfield sites, as catalysts of change in industrial relations.
3 It allows the trade union response to be understood.
4 It enables the changes to industrial relations since 1979, particularly in the car industry, to be understood.

Reports may opt for a unionized or non-union environment. In each case the following should be considered:

Unionized plant

• Which unions (and which employees may join).
• The process of selection.
• The contents of collective agreements (arbitration etc.).
• The organization of work.
• The strategy of the maintenance of management control.

Non-union plant

• Recruitment (whether to employ union members).
• Union prevention activities.
• Union substitution activities (grievance handling, employee communication).
• The strategy for the maintenance of management control.

Teaching style

The case can be used to introduce students, particularly business studies students, to industrial relations by looking at IR problems in terms of a strategic investment decision. However, the problem set is extremely complex and wide ranging, and the data presented in the case are deliberately sparse. Ancilliary data on the law, trade union structure, the car industry and on industrial relations elsewhere in the EEC would need to be provided to complete the consultants' reports.

The case has most frequently been used as the basis for group projects. It has been set in the first session of a course and approximately five weeks allowed for the group report and presentation, by which time students have more familiarity with the area. Five data packs, comprising academic articles and commercial data sources, have been provided, as follows:

1 Trade union organization in the UK, including the ACAS handbook, the TUC yearbook and the results of the latest workplace survey.
2 The legal background – including Incomes Data Services Handbooks and Briefs.
3 Background information on other EEC countries; primarily based on ILO publications and extracts from European Industrial Relations Review and Report.
4 A pack of collective agreements, containing 'no strike' deals and several examples from the car industry.
5 Data on the UK car industry, including Economist Intelligence Unit Reports, figures from the industry association, and the Marsden *et al.* volume.

References

P. Buckley, and P. Enderwick, *The industrial relations practices of foreign owned firms in Britain*, (Macmillan, 1985).

F. K. Foulkes, *Personnel Policies in Large Non-Union Companies*, (Prentice Hall, 1980).

'Group Working and Greenfield Sites', Incomes Data Services no. 314, May 1984.

D. Marsden *et al.*, *The Car Industry; Labour Relations and Industrial Adjustment*, (Tavistock, 1985).

'No Strike Deals in Perspective', Industrial Relations Review and Report, no. 324, July 1984.

'Nissan; A Deal for Teamwork and Flexibility?' Industrial Relations Review and Report, no. 344, May 1985.

J. Purcell, 'A Strategy for Control in Industrial Relations' in J. Purcell and R. Smith [eds.], *The Control of Work*, (Macmillan, 1979).

J. Purcell, and K. Sissons, 'Strategies and Practice in the Management of Industrial Relations' in G. Bain [ed.], *Industrial Relations in Britain*, (Blackwell, 1983).

P. Willman, 'The Reform of Collective Bargaining and Strike Activity at BL Cars', *Industrial Relations Journal*, vol. 15, no. 2, 1984.

P. Willman, and G. Winch, *Innovation and Management Control; Labour Relations at BL Cars*, (Cambridge University Press, 1985).

TWENTY-SEVEN

Suspending quality circles: Alcan Plate Limited

JOHN BANK

Introduction

Quality circles exist in companies in over thirty-five different countries worldwide. Alcan Plate examines the launch of a quality circle programme in an aluminium plate company near Birmingham. It illuminates critical case principles in quality circle programmes.

By providing a negative model of a quality circle launch, the case encourages readers to beware of simplistic notions of starting up a quality circles programme without proper planning. Although the idea itself is quite simple, quality circles can be a profound and rewarding management intervention in the area of employee involvement. But the quality circles programme needs commitment from the board, top management, middle management and trade unions, as well as support from the base of the company to succeed.

Before beginning the case the management student should do some background reading on the history and development of quality circles from their birth in Japan in 1962 to the present. The reading should also include something about the core principles, such as voluntary membership and ownership, and the basic organization and structure of a quality circles programme.

A coordinator or steering committee of top managers, a corpus of middle managers as facilitators and the frontline supervisors as quality circle leaders are needed for a well structured programme.

A positive focus for the case can be developed by simply asking management students to draw up a detailed plan for *relaunching* the quality circle programme at Alcan Plate. To do so would require some basic knowledge of quality circle theory and practice.

Theory and background

The quality circles concept is a universal one with millions of people involved all over the world. Although quality circles first developed in Japan during the early 1960s, the approach is based on Western theories of management, notably Douglas McGregor's Theory Y (1960).

If properly introduced, quality circles represents part of a coherent managerial philosophy. It is not a stand-alone concept. It forms one aspect of employee involvement. Quality circles are an approach which allows employees to become more involved in the workings of their section or department by solving their own job-related problems in an organized way.

First, quality circles is an approach which allows people to get more involved, but puts no pressure on them to do so, in other words the approach is entirely voluntary at all levels of the organization. This principle of voluntariness is crucial to the success of quality circles. It is, however, not an easy thing to introduce and to manage, since it is such an unusual notion. In the working life of most employees one rather suspects that nothing is really voluntary, and yet quality circles *are*, but it takes more than a mere statement to make the principle a reality.

The second distinctive feature of the quality circles approach is that the people who join in are encouraged to solve their own job-related problems. When asked to state what problems affect them at work, most people tend to point to difficulties caused by other sections, departments, or people, rather than to things that lie within their own sphere of influence. This inevitably causes frustration. Quality circles overcome this major difficulty of participative problem-solving by introducing the combined ideas of 'no finger pointing' and 'put your own house in order'. By focusing on issues that they can influence, quality circles are in a much stronger position to get things done than if they spend their time trying to tell others what to do.

The third feature of the quality circles definition is that circles solve their problems in an organized way. They are given training in the skills of systematic and creative problem-solving and of working together effectively in a group. They are also taught how to collect data so that their ideas can be based on facts rather than opinions. The quality circles approach is probably the only approach which gives problem-solving training to non-supervisory staff. Training is a key part of the concept since it gives members the tools to do the job. It should be remembered that for most staff this will be the first time that they have been involved in such an activity that it would be very dangerous to assume that the requisite skills were already in place and ready to be used.

Launching quality circles is not nearly as simple as it appears at first. It needs to form a part of the philosophy of management of the organization, it must be voluntary, and it must focus on 'putting our own house in order'. Furthermore, training must be given to enable groups to engage in the problem-solving activity in an organized and professional way.

A working definition of a quality circle would include the following elements: a group of four to ten volunteers who work for the same first-line supervisor, and who meet together regularly to identify, analyse and solve their work problems (Robson 1983).

First, quality circles is a natural work-group approach as distinct from a taskforce or project process, both of which tend to be inter-departmental or a vertical slice of the organization.

Second, the group does not need to consist of the entire workforce from that section. If twenty people work in an area and nine volunteer, then the nine form the quality circle. Of course, the remaining eleven must be kept informed at all times about the topics being tackled and indeed they should be encouraged to put forward their ideas even if they do not want to join the group.

Third, the groups meet regularly once a week, for an hour, and as far as possible in paid time. Once a week is a good practical balance between the desire to get on with things on the one hand, and the need to ensure that the workflow in the section is not adversely affected on the other. The meetings should be limited in length as an antidote to Parkinson's Law, and experience shows that an hour is the right length of time in most circumstances. The meetings should be held in paid time. This is because the meetings are about work, not leisure, and as such should be paid in the normal way; no more, no less.

Fourth, the groups do not stop at the identification of a problem for passing on to management to solve. They utilize the training they receive to analyse and solve it, and then to present their findings to management.

What are the objectives of a quality circles programme? There are three main goals,

1　Employee involvement.
2　People development.
3　The generation of tangible benefits.

The quality circles concept is one of the best mechanisms for encouraging direct employee involvement. Like work reorganization, it is a way of giving people more participation in decisions and more say over their work at the job level.

The second objective is the development of people in the organization. Quality circles undoubtedly promote the development of employees through the acquisition of new skills and the opportunity to work together on real problems. The quality circles training also helps supervisors to build their problem-solving skills and their abilities in working in, and leading, small groups. For many managers, quality circles offer the practical framework for introducing and developing genuinely participative management styles. Often, in the past, well-meaning attempts by managers to do this have foundered for want of a usable, practical framework and after a few months, 'participation' has been relegated to the side lines with the comment that it 'sounds all right in theory but . . .' Quality circles change this. Although based on sound theoretical premises, the approach is intensely practical. It builds the bridge back from theory to the real world.

The third goal of quality circles is to generate benefits for the organization and the people in it. The evidence suggests that quality circles programmes tend to be cost-effective and sometimes very much so. Research done in the UK in 1985 quotes a conservative payback of four times the investment, and often higher payback figures are reported. A vital concern about this, however, is that it is very dangerous to make this objective the primary one, since doing so will involve putting pressure on and maybe breaking some of the rules, notably that the groups 'own' the problem-selection process, and there should be no pressure on them to select one which is likely to generate direct tangible benefits. If this happens, the ownership of the group has been 'stolen' and the concept becomes nothing more than another management controlled and regulated technique.

Quality circles is an exciting, invigorating and fresh concept, but it is not a magic wand. If introduced with care and skill, however, it can contribute to the development of more healthy and effective organizations, in which people's abilities at all levels are recognized and valued, and where there is an opportunity provided for latent talent to be used.

A programme of introduction for quality circles

The introduction of quality circles can usefully be viewed in the five stages outlined below:

Stage 1   Planning and communication
At the outset of any programme it is necessary to devise a detailed plan of introduction. This will include the answers to such questions as the number of circles to introduce, arrangements for resourcing and the

timing of the programme. During the first stage communication meetings are held with managers, supervisors and unions to discuss the concept, gain agreement to its introduction, and to outline the overall plan.

Stage 2   Facilitator training

The key tasks of this stage are to identify the facilitators, train them in the requisite skills of developing people, counselling and problem-solving, and to develop a broad plan of their involvement. This will involve a training programme, depending on the needs of the organization, of between two and five days.

Stage 3   Leader training

The leader training course is a three-day programme during which the participants are given a thorough grounding in the knowledge and skills required to enable them to fulfil the role of a quality circle leader. This training involves learning about what happens in these kind of groups, so that the leader will be able to ensure that the meetings are well conducted. There is also a need for the leader to learn how to draw out the best from the members of the group. Finally there is the vital area of the problem-solving structure and techniques. The leader needs to understand these techniques and to have had the opportunity of practising them.

Stage 4   Getting started

Here the focus is on two key aspects of a successful programme:

1   Ensuring the circles are set up well and trained thoroughly. We recommend that organizations should plan to start with between two and six groups. The work at this stage involves:
   - Assisting with the presentations to potential circle members.
   - 'On the job' development of circle leaders as they set up and begin to run their groups.
   - Continuing development of facilitator skills in helping circles to move towards self-sufficiency.
2   Tackling the possible problem of some managers being sceptical. This involves:
   - Assisting circles to see the need to take this into account.
   - Helping circles to make it easy for managers to 'buy in'.
   - Holding communication meetings with managers.
3   A criticism sometimes made of quality circles states that they are something the top of the organization tells the middle to do to the bottom (Lawler 1985). A conscious effort to make management

support genuine and *visible* at all levels in the organization can help offset this concern.

Stage 5   Consolidation and expansion
During this stage the programme must be consolidated and the next phase of expansion planned and implemented. This will involve the following tasks:

- Ensuring that each circle completes its first problem–solving round, culminating in a management presentation.
- Helping the groups to identify their next subjects.
- Planning the extension of the programme with the coordinator.
- Starting up the next round of quality circles using internal resources.
- Continuing to ensure the development of management support.

'During the start-up phase, few serious threats to the programme arise. The worst are an insufficient number of volunteers, inadequate training, inability of volunteers to learn the procedures and, finally, lack of funding for meetings, facilitator times and training' (Lawler 1985).

One of the primary aims of quality circles is to re-establish the essential role of the foreman. It is important that he assumes leadership of the quality circles and helps shape it through careful project selection and training. Over the last sixty years the role of first line production supervisors has undergone extensive changes. Previously he exercised a good measure of control over the workforce and a rather straightforward relationship with his own supervisors. Today, the front line supervisor finds himself further removed from the decision-making centre that directly affects shopfloor and departmental work. The supervisory role has been viewed as 'man in the middle' (Roethlisberger 1945), who has to deal with the conflicting demands of management and the workers, or what has been called 'marginal men', occupying a position on the boundary between management and labour in a sort of organizatio-nal limbo (Wray 1949). Much of the research done on the superintendent was downward-looking from his position in the organization, focusing on his relationship with subordinates and the effects of his behaviour on workers' performance. An alternative perspective, that is viewing the supervisory role looking upwards, his relationship with higher management, reveals further changes in the role touching on his authority and the priorities which are set for him in terms of work objectives (Child 1975). Against the background of these unsettling changes, quality circles might result in a simple, clear method of asserting the foreman's leadership at the grass roots level by increasing participation and control. He is not only leader of the circle, but he assumes a training role as well with regard to circle members (Bank and Wilpert 1983).

Key learning points

1   Although anyone in the organization can *sponsor* the introduction of quality circles into the company, the *coordinator* of the programme should be a senior manager at the heart of the business (usually a line manager) who has a high profile and high credibility across the organization. *Facilitators* should be middle managers and quality circle leaders should be front line supervisors.
2   Sponsors, other senior managers, the coordinator, facilitators, quality circle leaders and members all need some training geared to quality circle techniques and procedures.
3   Companies should do as much of the training for quality circles as they can competently do. Starting with a pilot programme they should aim to 'grow' the programme themselves. However, they should also provide resources for as much outside consultancy as needed to ensure a correct launch and proper development of the programme.
4   Certain core quality circle principles should be adhered to. These include 'voluntarism at all levels, adequate training, a tight problem-solving focus for the work groups, the use of facilitators, presentations to the relevant levels of management and recognition'.
5   There exists a body of data which illuminates why quality circles fail (Bartlett). A study of the common reason for failure can lead to pre-emptive measures being taken in a quality circles launch and development.

Coordinator

While the sponsor of a quality circle programme – the 'champion' who introduces it into the company because he believes in the idea and is prepared to promote it – can come from anywhere in the organization, the *coordinator* who volunteers to administer the programme, should be a senior manager who is well respected in the company and who is at the centre of the business. He should normally be a line manager rather than someone with a staff function. In a warehousing operation, he might be the traffic manager, in an engineering works he could be the production manager, in a retail operation he could be the marketing manager. His role includes the following activities:

- Focal point.
- Programme administrator.
- Communications.
- Plan the future – make decisions.
- Uphold principles.

The facilitator's role includes:

- Make groups self-sufficient:
    training
    development.
- 'Process' not 'task'.
- Develop leader:
    confidence
    competence.
- Make it easy for others to:
    understand
    support
    'buy in'.
- Oil wheels.

The quality circle leader's role encompasses the following roles:

- Trainer of quality circle members.
- Helps members feel comfortable in the meeting situation.
- Ensures that there is no elitism among quality circle members and that they stay in touch with the work group.
- Ensures that quality circles keep a problem-solving focus and stick to problems in the work group.
- Make it easy for others to co-operate with or join the quality circle.

Training

The investigators of quality circles at Alcan assumed that no specific quality circle training was needed for anyone in the company. The quality circle leaders were given a few pointers on chairmanship. No systematic problem-solving training was provided for facilitators, circle leaders or circle members.

Whether this decision was made as an economy measure or simply due to a misunderstanding of the classic model one cannot tell. But the consequences of no training took its toll on the programme.

All practitioners 'In addition to the training for facilitators and leaders, others in the organization generally benefit from learning more about the quality circle process. Training programmes for managers including middle management and union officials, are the ideal way to expose them to the quality circle concept' (Bartlett).

Role of the outside consultant

The Alcan managers decided to avoid both training and outside consultants. Going it alone meant that there was no expertise to help them avoid their mistakes and no specific quality circle training for anyone in the company. Had there been a quality circle expert working with the installation of the programme many costly mistakes could have been avoided.

The external quality circle consultant offers the company six important benefits.

1 He provides objectivity about the intervention.
2 He brings 'state-of-the-art' technology to the quality circle launch.
3 He underwrites uncertainties for management in that he has helped other companies launch quality circle programmes and knows the elephant traps.
4 He acts as a catalyst for ideas and action in this employee involvement effort.
5 He provides extra working capacity provided for the specific objectives of launching and developing the quality circle programme.
6 He provides facilitator and leader training.

Core principles

The case demonstrates how a company runs into great difficulties with a quality circle start up if they neglect the core principles which have proven essential to quality circle programmes everywhere. For example, Alcan made a general foreman instead of foremen the quality circle leaders, which was one level higher than front-line supervisors. The immediate supervisors of the general foreman, the superintendents, sat in on the meetings which certainly could have been interpreted as a lack of trust in the general foreman's leadership. It could have set up a rivalry for leadership and would have daunted most foremen.

Initial problems were given to the Alcan quality circles by the superintendents 'to help get them started' which adversely affected the quality circle's ownership of the problems and violated the core principle that quality circles identify, analyse and solve problems of their own choosing.

By having quality circles dependent on managers at too high a level in the organization Alcan created difficulties for the circles. When teething problems were encountered with the new furnaces and the new computers that made unrelenting demands on these managers, keeping them from attending the quality circles meetings, the meetings were cancelled. Momentum fell and eventually when large-scale redundancies added to the managers' problems, the quality circle programme was suspended.

Why quality circles fail

The case contains some explicit data from America as to why quality circles fail. Such frequent indicators of failure should be studied, contrasted and compared with research from other countries. A coincidence in the data indicate that just as there are universal core principles for quality circles there are also common causes of failure (Dale and Howard).

A survey of sixty-seven British companies published in 1984, for example, stated that the main reasons for failures include rejection of the concept by top management and trade unions, the disruption caused by redundancies and company restructuring, labour turn-over, lack of cooperation from middle and first-line management, and failure by circle leaders to find enough time to organize meetings.

As the case bears out most of these problems affected the quality circle launch at Alcan. The research also clearly indicates that, as at Alcan Plate, when there is a quality circle failure or suspension of the programme, the vast majority are willing to try again.

Teaching style

Start with a small group discussion in separate places. Use flipcharts within groups. Have each group summarize on the flipcharts their discussion of how they would plan a *relaunch* of quality circles at Alcan Plate.

At the plenary session ask each group to present its findings.

Tutors should update the research in the case on quality circle failures and discuss localized data, if it exists. They could then broaden discussions to the position of quality circles in the field of employee involvement.

References

J. Bank, and B. Wilpert, 'What's So Special About Quality Circles?', *Journal of General Management*, Autumn 1983, vol. 9, no. 1, pp. 25 and 26.

J. B. Bartlett, *Success and Failure in Quality Circles – A Study of 25 Companies*, London Employee Relations Resource Centre.

B. Dale, and S. Hayward, *A Study of Quality Circle Failures*, Manchester, UMIST.

E. E. Lawler, and S. A. Mohrman, 'Quality Circles after the fad', *Harvard Business Review*, January/February 1985, p. 67.

D. McGregor, *The Human Side of Enterprise*, (McGraw-Hill, 1960).

W. Mohr, and H. Mohr, *Quality Circles: Changing Images of People at Work*, (Addison Wesley Publishing, Menlo Park, California, 1983), p. 62.

M. Robson, *Quality Circles: A Practical Guide*, (Gower Publishing, 1983).

Index

Administration, orders of, 210–11
Analytical skills, 35–6, 37
Appraisal interviews, 35, 36
  tutorial styles, 40–1

Business unit strategy, 113–14

Causal-analytic interview style, 40, 41
Change agent, role of internal, 53–4
Client identification, 124–5
Cohort analysis, 178
Communication failures, 70, 72
Communication skills, 11, 36, 149–50
Consultants:
  ethics, 124–5
  internal, 53–4
  intervention by, 115–16, 120, 126
  quality circle, 238
Consultation meetings, 65
Contracting/shrinking organization, 8
Control systems, 209–12
Co-ordinator, role of, 236–7
Core principles, quality circle, 238
Corporate strategy, 113–14, 170
Culture, organizational, 52–3, 72, 123

Data feedback, 134–43
  model, 142
Decision making, 111–13
Delegation, 65

Development problems, 10
Directive interview style, 40, 41
Dynamic approach, 19

Effort/wage bargain, 217
Employment conditions, 203

Facilitator, role of, 237
Factor comparison schemes, 190
Fiddles, piecework, 211, 217
Foreman, role of, 235–6
Forming stage, group, 97–8

Grade drift, 188
Group interactions, 98, 101, 102, 103
Group norms, 59–60
Group selection procedures, 204

'Hands on' management style, 63
Hostility and conflict, 48
Human resource management, 9, 171

Incremental approach, 112
Induction crisis, 178
Industrial relations strategies, 226–8
Information, need for, 135
Internal drives, 3
Interpersonal behaviour:
  barriers, 97, 99
  communications, 25
  perceptions, 28
  senior management level, 48
  skills, 35, 37

Interview process, 37–9

Job description, 202
Job evaluation schemes, 189–91
Job satisfaction, 5

Labour turnover rate, 177–8
Leadership style, 17, 19, 21, 97, 99,
    102, 103

Management development, 9, 13,
    62, 65, 146, 194–7
Management style examples,
    157–65
Management team performance,
    95–6, 96–105
Managerial redundancies, 9
Managerial work analysis, 63
Managing change, 169
Manpower demand forecasting, 177
Middle manager's role, 62
Miscommunications, 70–2
Motivational process, 3, 5, 10

Needs and motivation, 4
Negotiating deals, 51
Normative thinking, 111–12
'Norming' stage, group, 98–100
'Norming/storming' cycle, 101–2
Norms of behaviour, 59–60

Organizational behaviour (OB), 153
Organizational culture, 52–3, 159
Organizational development, 12
Organizational influence, 97, 100,
    102, 104
Output limitation, 215–16

Peer pressure effect, 59–60
People development programme
    (PDP), 83
Perception process, 28
Performance annual review (PAR),
    85
Performance criteria, 52
Performance equation, 7
Performing stage, 103

'Person orientated' manager, 22, 23
Personality influence, 64, 99
Personnel management role, 182–5
Piecework strategies, 217–19
Points schemes, job evaluation, 190
Political activity, 9, 12–13, 48, 49
Positional opportunities and
    constraints, 49–50
Power play, 23, 24
Power struggle concept, 210
Problem identification, 136
Product strategy team (PST), 82
'Production orientated' manager,
    22, 23
Profit improvement programme
    (PIP), 78
Promotion opportunities, creating,
    9
Promotional blockage, 12

Quality circles, 230–9

Rationality, belief in, 51
Recruitment and selection process,
    200–1
Reorganization processes, 160–5
Reward structures, 188–9

Salary policies, 189
Self-motivation, 5, 150
Senior management styles, 22
Sensitivity (to issues), 11
Situational leadership, 25
Smoothing strategies, 137–8
Social action control systems, 210
Socialization process, 57
Socio-technical control systems,
    209–10
Stakeholder analysis, 50–1, 122, 126
'Storming' stage, group, 98–100
Strategic management, 200
Strategy, formation of, 111–13, 125
Subordinates, understanding, 11
Supervisory responsibilities, 149
SWOT analysis (strengths,
    weaknesses, opportunities,
    threats), 170

Index

Tactics, 124, 125
Team development, 95–6
    wheel, 96–7, 108
Third party facilitators, 120–1
Time and motion expert, 19
Total quality concept, 92–5
Trade union structures, 221–4

Tutoring styles, alternative, 41

WASP recruitment approach, 200–1
Wastage rates, labour, 178
Whole job ranking schemes, 189
Work group solidarity, 211
Work/wage bargain, 217